Healthcare Value Selling

Winning Strategies to Sell and Defend Value in the New Market

Christopher D. Provines

Published by the Healthcare Value Institute LLC.

DEDICATION

To my family: Dee, Andrew, Christopher, Erin, and, last but not least, Murphy—I couldn't have done it without you.

CONTENTS

LIST OF FIGURES

LIST OF TABLES

ACKNOWLEDGMENTS

The Chinese philosopher Lao-Tzo said that a journey of a thousand miles begins with one step. Much like a long journey, writing a book is a long process that begins with one word or idea. It's a journey that requires the support of many people to finish.

Over the course of twenty-four years working in healthcare, I have had the good fortune to work in excellent organizations—both healthcare providers and suppliers. These organizations were filled with talented and insightful people from whom I learned much.

Likewise, as an instructor and consultant, I've had the gift of being able to work with outstanding organizations and people. Over the years, I've had the opportunity to train thousands of executives and students. Smart instructors realize that each class presents a great opportunity to share what you've learned, but also to pick up new ideas and insights. I'm grateful to the students who have challenged me and provided new insights.

In a way, the work, consulting, and training experiences prepared me for the journey of writing this book. Collectively, these insights are captured here.

Some individuals provided specific support during the development of this book. I'm grateful for the advice and support of Tom Reynolds, Mike Reiner, Jason Aroesty, John Phillips, Ravi Avva, John Ure, Russ Procopio, and Steve Haggett. I thank my wife, Dee Provines, for her advice on book cover designs. Finally, I thank my editor, Kristen Ebert-Wagner, who made the final product so much better than the rough draft.

PREFACE

Why another book on selling or negotiating? Amazon.com is filled with books on these two topics. They come in different colors and sizes—and often sport catchy titles. I'm not knocking these books. I have a bunch on my bookshelf and Kindle. Most are excellent.

This book was born from experience and need. Many years ago, while working for a large healthcare company, I took on a project to help the organization better sell its value. The company offered great solutions, but there was a belief that the sales team could do a better job of selling value.

By value, I don't mean the fluffy stuff. Value means quantifying the unique financial impact of your solution on the customer's business. At the time, I conducted research, interviewed many people, and bought a lot of books.

Unfortunately, there wasn't a practical and comprehensive set of books on selling value. Some were academic. Others told compelling stories but provided little guidance for implementing the ideas. None of the books answered the simple question, how do I sell and defend value? Moreover, none addressed the nuances of selling and defending value in the healthcare market.

Eventually, we rolled out selling tools that helped us quantify the value of our solutions. After all, this was what many of the books said you had to do. You needed to quantify value and give the sales team a tool. Following the roll-out of tools, I learned the hard way that creating a value tool is the easy part.

There were many unanswered questions we needed to address to make this work:

- When in the sales process—or, more important, the customer buying process—do I use this tool?

- How do I introduce the information from the tool to educate the customer?

- The tool is solution-centric; how do I first educate the customer about the problem?

- How do I handle financial questions and objections from the financial buyer?

- The sales force is trained to sell clinically. How do we get them comfortable with the business side?

- How do different reimbursement models impact the value story?

- The purchasing guy says he doesn't care about my value story. What do I do now?

- Our product has become a commodity. How is this possibly going to help?

- The tender is already written. What do we do now?

I'm not trying to make this complicated. This is the reality. These are all good questions. If you can't answer these questions and some others, then merely developing a value tool and giving it to sales may be of limited worth.

Why bother with value? Healthcare in the United States, and many parts of the world, is undergoing a fundamental shift. The days of selling primarily on clinical benefits are over. If you can't translate the unique financial impact of your solution for the customer's business, you will not succeed in the future. Moreover, you need to educate and convince the customer of the unique value you bring as a supplier.

Reimbursement reforms, evolving evidence requirements, buying committees, accountable care organizations (ACOs), and value-based purchasing are just some of the drivers of change. These are causing a fundamental shift in how goods and services are purchased. For many suppliers, it may feel like a new market.

Beyond these drivers, there is a long-term trend of hospital supply chains becoming more sophisticated. This means your customers are going to become smarter buyers. The Corporate Executive Board, the group behind the *Challenger Sale* book, conducted research showing that customers complete nearly 60 percent of a typical purchasing decision before even having a conversation with a supplier.

As someone who has worked in procurement, I see this change in the buying process as being driven by the rise of professional buyers. If you understand the professional buyers' process, it will become clear that they are the key driver behind this statistic. Transparency, driven by the Internet, is also helping to drive this change. However, in larger, sophisticated organizations, purchasing or materials management is the key driver.

The title of this book brings together two important concepts. Selling value means using your quantified value to help educate and influence the customer. Studies show that even among the most sophisticated buyers, only a third regularly quantify value in order to make purchasing decisions.

Defending your value is becoming equally important. The rise of professional buyers and the growing sophistication of healthcare supply chains means that sellers will need to be able to handle these tough buyers. Smart sellers need to understand buyers' tactics and, more important, why buyers use these tactics and how to combat them.

This book leverages twenty-four years of eclectic experience in healthcare. This includes experience working on the other side of the table in hospital finance and reimbursement, and a leadership role in procurement. Understanding the customer side of selling and negotiating is critical as professional buyers play a more important role in buying decisions. This book approaches selling and defending value from the customer's perspective.

In addition, I gathered insights from years of experience rolling out value selling programs in large healthcare businesses, and experience in pricing and healthcare economics, in account management and commercial excellence, and in training thousands of salespeople.

As a part-time academic, I've been interested in the evolution of the healthcare supply chains and market. This book is also based on significant research on the evolving healthcare buyer, including interviews with economic buyers, research on the evolving provider supply chain, study of ACOs, review of the impact of reimbursement reforms on buying, and study of buying processes and tactics in healthcare.

This book is intended for sales and marketing teams in healthcare. More specifically, it is geared primarily to people selling goods and services to providers. Providers are hospitals, surgical centers, and other entities that deliver healthcare. It also addresses the nuances of selling value to ACOs.

The intended audience is those in sales who deal with the economic buyers. Depending on the supplier organization structure, these salespeople could be working in corporate accounts, sales management, or market access or may sometimes be frontline sales professionals.

While this book focuses heavily on selling and defending value at the moment of execution in the field, others in healthcare supplier organizations will benefit from the tools and insights here. Specifically, marketing teams should find the ideas and tools helpful. Much like sales, marketing teams at many suppliers are trying to evolve in response to the new market.

More important, real success in selling and defending value requires that sales and marketing work together. The marketing team needs to build the value stories and make the right investments in evidence to support value selling. Furthermore, the marketing team needs to carefully consider the offering strategy and design offerings that allow sales to defend value.

This book is also, admittedly, skewed to the US form of healthcare. Each country has a different healthcare system and structure. Selling value in Finland will be different from selling value in Spain, which will be different from selling value in the US and Korea. Addressing all of these variations and nuances in a single book would be tough on the author—and probably the readers as well!

Yet, even in different markets, many of the basic principles and concepts in this book will still be relevant. Some of the trends that are impacting the US market hold true for markets in Europe, Asia, and Latin America. Customer consolidation, the growing power of economic buyers, and the need to quantify and communicate value are all common themes. Whether you are selling in Brazil, India, or the US, these themes and trends are impacting these markets.

All of the changes happening in healthcare at the moment make it a complicated and challenging time. This book is intended to make the complex simple, and at the same time to provide the content necessary to help commercial teams and salespeople transition to the new world. I hope you agree that the book has found the right balance.

PART I

INTRODUCTION AND CONTEXT

Chapter | 1

INTRODUCTION: A QUESTION OF VALUE

What is a cynic? A man who knows the price of everything and the value of nothing.

—Oscar Wilde[1]

Do customers even care about value? A common complaint heard from salespeople is that more and more it feels like the only thing customers care about is price. Despite valiant efforts to communicate value, the buying decision often seems to come back to price. So why bother with value?

Read the results of any survey of what's important to the customer in a buying decision, and you will often see price show up after factors like quality, delivery, training, and support. Moreover, talk to any procurement person or read their books on strategic sourcing, and you will hear that price should not be the top buying factor.

So what's going on here? How can price appear to be the primary focus of buyers when surveys show that price is not one of the top buying considerations? There can only be a limited number of explanations for these different perspectives:

- *The customer really doesn't care about value.* For a variety of reasons, some customers really do care only about price. It could be how they view the supply category. On the other hand, the customer may simply be facing tremendous short-term financial pressure, and be willing to take the risk of using a lower-cost, lower-quality supplier.

3

- *It's a negotiation tactic.* Customers are becoming increasingly sophisticated buyers. It could be that the customer has learned to focus on price as a negotiation tactic to get suppliers to lower their prices.

- *There are no perceived value differences.* The customer may see no real difference in value between your solution and the next best alternative. So price is the deciding buying factor. This, of course, doesn't mean that the solutions are the same. It only means that this is the customer's perception. The lack of a perceived difference could be because the customer doesn't believe you. As one hospital chief financial officer said, almost every vendor is promising savings, but often the savings never materialize.[2]

- *You're not aligned with the buying process.* All customers have a process for buying goods and services. It starts with problem or opportunity recognition. Later, their buying process moves on to developing a sourcing strategy and negotiating with suppliers. If you engage at the wrong time in the buying process or engage in the wrong way, there's no hope of getting your message across.

- *You're talking to the wrong person.* Maybe the person you are selling to has a personal incentive to reduce costs and doesn't care about value differences. If this is the case, you need to find someone who does.

Sorting through all of this can be a challenge. Often it's not obvious what is happening. This is particularly true as the buying decision evolves, and as committees and purchasing play a more important role in the buying process.

Is the customer playing a negotiating game, or do they really only care about price? Is your value story effective? Does it supply the evidence required? Are you using it at the right stage of the customer's buying process? Are you talking to the wrong person? Who should you be talking with? These are all good questions, and ones that will be addressed in this book. Let's start with the question of value.

PERSPECTIVES ON VALUE

Everyone Talks Value

At a recent conference held between healthcare suppliers and group purchasing organization (GPO) executives, a supplier representative observed that customers always talk about total cost of ownership (TCO) or value, but that ultimately these always seem to be trumped by price. His point was that all customers seem to care about is price, not value.[3]

A GPO executive responded insightfully. This is paraphrasing, but he said that "product benefit claims made by new suppliers are a dime a dozen. We hear it every day. If I were a supplier, I would be doing everything in my power to build a highly differentiated value proposition—something designed to get our attention. Something novel that recognizes I see salesmen hawking 'the latest and greatest' every day. Perhaps a creative presentation that provides me with clear, concise, documented evidence of TCO versus the typically well-intended, but unsubstantiated claims—that would be a great start. Perhaps an actual plan that spells out the sought-after collaboration versus a commitment to figure it out later."[4]

This exchange offers a couple of interesting insights. Basically, the GPO executive was saying, "Stop coming in with your weak value stories that lack evidence." Or, more directly, "Stop wasting my time!" He was also saying, "Real supplier–customer relationships should be a collaboration. Therefore, please have a plan for collaborating with me if you are a serious supplier."

Most Suppliers Struggle to Quantify Value

I was presenting to a group of about a hundred professional buyers recently. I asked them, "How many of your suppliers actually quantify the value that their solution can or will bring to you?" About five people raised their hands.[5]

It's not that the purchasing people were shy. This is a typical response to this question. If you're in sales, just look in your own sales bag. Count the number of your key products or solutions that have a clear and compelling value proposition.

By value proposition, we're not talking about a long list of features. Features are facts or data about your product or solution. Features describe what the product or solution is, not what it does for the customer.

We are also not referring to benefits. Benefits describe how a feature of your product addresses a customer need. Benefits are better than features, but they are still not value. Value is about quantifying, in monetary terms, the differentiated benefit your solution provides.

Many Purchasers Can't Quantify Value Either

If you look at the other side of the negotiation table at purchasing or materials management, you might assume that they can quantify value for you if you are clear enough about your benefits. If you make this assumption, you are most likely wrong.

Studies show that only a third of the best-run purchasing organizations routinely calculate TCO or value for key supply decisions.[6] In the supply chain world, TCO means the cost to acquire, use, maintain, and dispose of a solution over some period. It's basically a measure of value. High-performing purchasing organizations use TCO analysis to help them make supplier decisions.

Professional Buyers Default to a Price Focus on Purpose

If you were a professional buyer, would you want your suppliers to think that price did not matter as a key decision factor? Of course you would want them to think price was very important. As one professional buyer said in an interview, "I pick out which supplier I want in advance. It is usually the higher-value, high-priced supplier. I then add a lot of other suppliers into the bid to drive my preferred supplier's prices down. It usually works."[7]

While it may seem like price is the most important factor in the buying decision, it usually isn't. Professional buyers often try to get you to concentrate on price during negotiations in order to persuade you to lower your price. Some buyers are very coercive and dishonest about this, and others are more balanced.

This leads to why this book is about selling *and* defending value. It is not enough to be able to quantify your value and use it in the right ways during the sales process. While this is a great start, it is necessary but not sufficient. You also have to be able to negotiate, or defend your value.

Negotiating, or defending value, is becoming more important because of the changes in the buying process. One of the drivers of this is the rise of professional buyers and the maturing of the hospital supply chain. In the future, more and more of the supply base will be controlled or influenced by professional buyers. So, if you're in sales, you should get prepared.

FOUR BASIC PRINCIPLES—SELL AND DEFEND VALUE

Throughout this book we will cover many tools, techniques, and approaches to selling and defending value. Beyond these approaches, it's helpful to keep some principles in mind. Some of these may seem basic. However, just like in sports, it's often the discipline to do the basic, fundamental things well that can make all the difference in the results.

Principle 1—Start with a Collaborative Mind-set

Some books and trainers teach salespeople to approach the customer as if entering a battle. This is particularly true with advice given to salespeople for dealing with purchasing or materials management organizations. Your customer is not your enemy. Even the most difficult person you have to work through in purchasing is not your enemy.

These professional buyers simply have a job to do. They have goals, targets, and objectives just like you. Sure, some of them can be really difficult or may, at times, seem unethical. However, most are just doing their job. If you better understand their job and how they think, you'll have a much better time selling and negotiating.

Whether you are working with a clinician, someone in administration, or someone in materials management, remember the definition of collaboration: "to work with another person or group in order to achieve or do something."[8] Obviously, in order to collaborate, you have to know what the customer wants to achieve. In other words, you need to know their goals, objectives, metrics, and targets.

An experienced procurement leader told a story of collaboration that led to a breakthrough with a supplier.[9] An incumbent supplier, who provided a critical service to the procurement leader's company, scheduled a meeting with the procurement leader. The supplier asked what the procurement leader's goals were for the coming year.

This approach may sound pretty basic. Yet the procurement leader mentioned that this was the first time a supplier had asked him about his goals. Most of the time, salespeople tried to go around or hide from him. The fact that the supplier engaged in a meaningful dialogue about the procurement leader's goals and needs was novel.

The procurement leader explained that his company was facing some financial pressure. His biggest goal was to identify new ways to take costs out of the business. His company had already captured much of the low-hanging fruit in terms of sourcing initiatives. He now needed creative ways to reduce costs. Given the financial pressures, he also had a lot of support from his senior management to change the way business was done in order to save money.

The supplier posed a simple question—"If I help you find a way to take costs out, will you work with me to help me improve my profitability?" It seemed like a fair trade. Ultimately, the supplier was able to identify a new way to provide his services by changing the business model. He was able to outsource and automate parts of the service provided to the customer. This meant lower costs for the customer, but also higher profits for the supplier.

A collaborative mind-set is a powerful tool. Now, sometimes customers will approach you with demands for a lower price. Their demands may seem like threats. The situation may feel very confrontational. In this case, it might not seem like the customer is interested in collaboration. In later chapters, we'll explore some powerful tools and techniques to handle situations like this. Just because the customer is taking an adversarial approach doesn't mean you should.

Asking the simple question of why the customer needs a lower price can lead to an opportunity. Sometimes the buyer may be completely upfront rather than play games. One procurement leader told about how he often makes a simple request of sellers. He asks them what he must do to reduce the seller's cost to serve. His expectation is that the cost savings will be passed on to him as lower prices. Rather than simply demand a lower price, he asks how they can collaborate.

He told of working with a supplier to eliminate unnecessary services like expedited delivery and other support. This allowed the supplier to lower his costs to serve and to pass these savings on to the customer in the form of lower prices. He accomplished this not by simply lowering the price but by changing his offering.

Many of the services provided weren't needed. In this case, the procurement person asked the supplier to tell him what he could do to lower the supplier's costs. If one of your key customers approached you with a request to eliminate unnecessary services and to lower your price, would you be ready to have that conversation?

This type of supplier–customer collaboration happens in many industries. It is relatively new to healthcare, but it could be a big opportunity in the future. We'll discuss the idea of flexible offerings and how to use these to your advantage in chapter 7.

Principle 2—Take The Other Side's Perspective for Better Results

We can define perspective-taking in many different ways. In his book, *To Sell Is Human*, Daniel Pink describes this as the ability to see the world from another person's perspective.[10] It means trying to think like the other side. In other words, it's about understanding their interests and motives. This is an important skill in negotiations.

Learning negotiation or sales techniques to deal with different selling scenarios is not enough. It's like a physician trying to treat a patient's symptoms rather than trying to understand the root causes of those symptoms. You have to try to get behind what the other side is doing or saying, and understand why they are doing or saying it. This means trying to understand the world from their perspective.

As an example of the power of this principle, researchers studied the effectiveness of perspective-taking and compared it with empathy as a strategy in negotiations. Empathy is the ability to connect emotionally with another individual. This skill is often considered important for salespeople.

The researchers conducted a series of experiments with groups of participants.[11] The experiments involved the sale and purchase of a gas station. They were purposefully set up so that price alone could not be negotiated. The negotiators would have to consider the other side's interests and bring these into the negotiation to find a solution.

The negotiators were split into three groups. One group was instructed to consider the other side's feelings while negotiating. In other words, they were told to empathize with the other side. Another group was told to consider the other side's perspective. This means putting oneself in the other person's shoes and thinking like they would think. The third group was a control group. The researchers conducted a series of experiments and compared the results.

It turns out that the group that was instructed to consider what the other side was thinking had better negotiation outcomes. They were able to find solutions more often. The results were mixed for the empathy group. Sometimes empathy led to suboptimal value exchange. It caused the negotiator to give up important self-interests in the negotiation, and to make too many concessions.

This principle of understanding what the other side is thinking is especially important when dealing with professional buyers. Many of their sourcing and negotiating tactics are designed to put the supplier on the defensive. If you understand their tactics and what they are thinking, you can put yourself in a much better position during the sales and negotiation process.

Principle 3—Keep It Simple

Throughout this book, you'll be given a number of tools, frameworks, and techniques for quantifying your value and using it in selling and negotiating. You'll also be given many tools for better understanding the customer's buying process and buying decision. These should prepare you well for selling and defending your value.

In practice, people tend to believe that adding more details to a value story will result in a more precise and persuasive story. This often leads companies to develop highly sophisticated and complex selling tools. The result can be a tool or messaging that even many in the company can't understand. More important, these tools or messages are often difficult to explain to the customer.

Buyers are busy. They don't have time to wade through complex spreadsheets or complicated calculations. You have to make it simple enough for them to understand and care. The GPO executive in the story at the beginning of the chapter said it well. He wanted "a creative presentation that provides me with clear, concise, documented evidence."

Keeping it simple really means forcing yourself and your company to make the value story as clear and concise as possible. This doesn't mean that your story should be overly simplified or lacking evidence. Rather, it means making clear to the decision makers exactly what the consequences are for using or not using your solution.

Principle 4—Prepare, Prepare, Prepare

Healthcare systems are under tremendous pressure to reduce costs and to improve quality. Payers are implementing new payment and reimbursement models to drive costs out, reduce unnecessary use of services, and improve outcomes and quality. This change in payment and reimbursement models is changing how providers view supplies and suppliers. Suppliers need to prepare for this new world.

Beyond the changes in the reimbursement models, many other factors are driving changes in healthcare. We will dive deep into these in the next chapter. Factors like the changing buying process, outcomes-based sourcing, and the evolving physician–hospital buying power are all changing how solutions are negotiated and purchased. Thus, suppliers will need to change how they sell and negotiate. More important, they must prepare in new ways.

Finally, the last key driver of change requiring suppliers to prepare is the evolution of the supply chain and professional buyers. As the name implies, a professional buyer is someone trained with tools and techniques to obtain the maximum possible value from the supply market. In the hospital market, these professional buyers may be called materials management, purchasing, strategic sourcing, or other names. They employ a range of tools, strategies, and tactics. The smart ones spend considerable time analyzing supply alternatives and preparing for negotiations.

As an example, the Corporate Executive Board, the group behind the *Challenger Sales* book, conducted research showing that customers complete nearly 60 percent of a typical purchasing decision—researching solutions, ranking options, setting requirements, benchmarking pricing, and so on—before even having a conversation with a supplier.[12] Professional buyers will tell you that much of this change in buying behavior is being driven by the strategic sourcing processes they're implementing.

All of these factors make preparation much more important. The days of getting physicians interested in your product, and then getting a product on contract, are largely over. The buying process is becoming more complex, and the buyers more sophisticated. As Benjamin Franklin observed, "by failing to prepare, you are preparing to fail."[13]

ORGANIZATION OF THE BOOK

This book is organized to provide the reader with a simple-to-follow, practical approach to selling and defending value. In the new world of healthcare, being able to quantify value and use it to educate the customer is necessary, but not sufficient. The rise of the professional buyer and the maturing of supply chains means that successful salespeople will need to be able to negotiate and defend value as well. The material is organized in five key sections. Figure 1.1 provides an overview of the structure of the book and shows how these sections fit together into a cohesive framework.

Figure 1.1. Selling and defending value

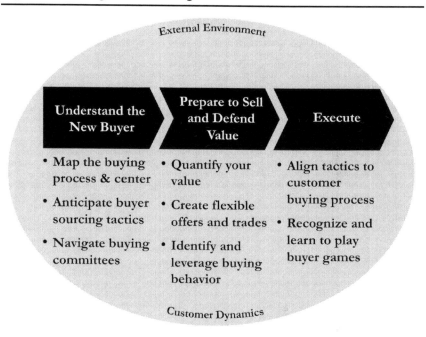

- **Part I: Introduction and Context.** This part provides some big-picture framing of why suppliers need to become skilled at selling and defending value. Once you fully understand the trends and changes taking place in healthcare, it will be clear that salespeople, and the people who support sales, need to adapt to the new world in order to be the winners.

- **Part II: Understand the New Buyer.** For salespeople and sales teams who have been selling based on clinical features and benefits, it's critical to understand the new buyer. This includes understanding professional buyers and their sourcing tactics. It also includes mapping the buying process and buying center. Finally, it's about being able to successfully navigate buying committees.

- **Part III: Prepare to Sell and Defend Value.** This section covers three critical topics. First, it shows you how to quantify your value. This is not the mushy value proposition that the GPO executive said was a waste of his time in the story at the beginning of the chapter. In this section, I show you how to quantify value in monetary terms that matter to buyers. Next, I show you how to develop offers and trades. These are key tools to use when negotiating with professional buyers. Finally, I share a way to think about hospital buying behavior and how to link your strategies to this buying behavior.

- **Part IV: Sell and Defend Value.** In this section, I explore how to put your value, trades, and knowledge to work. This includes aligning your value tactics with where the customer is in the buying process. I also discuss the important topic of how to recognize and play buyer games. Even the most honest, well-intended supply-chain professional will admit to playing a few games with suppliers. They do this because it works! Don't fall for these buyer games.

- **Part V: Appendices.** The appendices provide more detail on two important areas related to selling and defending value. Appendix A addresses reimbursement and includes a review of the related basic terms and mechanisms. Appendix B addresses accountable care organizations (ACOs). ACOs are a relatively new entity in the US, and it's important for suppliers to understand ACOs as well as how ACOs view value. Because healthcare continues to evolve, both of these topics provide a basic foundation for the reader to build on.

USING THIS BOOK

The book is organized in a logical sequence. It builds on the foundational elements and then moves to execution. However, not everyone needs the same level of depth and coverage in the various topics. Therefore, you should use the tools and sections that make the most sense for you and your business.

To get the most out of this book, you should practice applying the concepts to your business. Usually this works best with a group of people. While you can certainly apply many of the tools yourself, working with a group to brainstorm, debate, and discuss almost always elevates the quality of the thinking. These tools and frameworks make for great exercises at regional or national sales meetings.

This book is not intended to offer legal, regulatory, or marketing advice. It presents concepts, tools, and examples to help you think about your own situation. However, each healthcare market adheres to different laws and regulations. In addition, rules and laws surrounding the promotion of healthcare products and services are always evolving. It is up to you to seek appropriate legal, regulatory, and other professional counsel when selling and marketing your products and services. I make no claims as to the suitability of the ideas, examples, or tools to any specific situation.

Finally, readers should not misconstrue the purpose of the tools and concepts in this text. Given all the pressure that healthcare systems face, providers around the world need to reduce costs and improve the quality of care. This book is intended to help suppliers support their customers in making better purchasing decisions. It is also intended to help suppliers get paid fairly for the value they create.

KEY TAKEAWAYS

- The healthcare system is rapidly evolving, and value will be the key buying factor. To sell and defend your value, you will need a new level of skills and knowledge.

- There are many reasons why a customer will say that price is the most important buying factor. Understanding and sorting through this is critical to successfully selling and defending your value.

- Beyond the tools and techniques explained throughout the book, you should remember the basic principles of selling and defending value.

- These principles include being collaborative, keeping it simple, taking the other side's perspective, and preparing for success.

NOTES

1. www.brainyquote.com (accessed November 2, 2013).

2. C. Provines, "Smart Purchasing: Evolving Hospital Buying and Implications for Suppliers" (Working paper, 2014).

3. T. Finn, "Is Selling Total Cost of Ownership (TCO) a Waste of Time?" *Healthcare Matters,* HCMatters.com, October 26, 2012 (accessed November 3, 2013).

4. Ibid.

5. C. Provines, "How the Supply Base Is Moving to Value-Based Competition & How Procurement Should Prepare," presentation at NextLevel Purchasing Conference, September 13, 2013.

6. Based on a Hackett Group study. Cited in A. All, "Procurement Must Look Beyond 'Stuff' to Strategy," *IT Business Edge,* July 2007 (accessed January 16, 2010).

7. C. Provines, "Professional Buyers' View of Suppliers" (Unpublished manuscript, 2013).

8. Merriam Webster Online Dictionary, http://www.merriam-webster.com/ (accessed November 3, 2013).

9. Provines, "Professional Buyers' View of Suppliers."

10. Daniel Pink, *To Sell Is Human* (Riverhead Trade, 2013).

11. This idea was developed from Pink, *To Sell Is Human.* The original research comes from A. D. Galinsky, W. W. Maddux, D. Gilin, and J. B. White, "Why It Pays to Get Inside the Head of Your Opponent: The Differential Effects of Perspective Taking and Empathy in Negotiations," *Psychological Science* 19.4 (April 2008): 378–84.

12. B. Adamson, M. Dixon, and N. Toman, "The End of Solution Selling," *Harvard Business Review, HBR.org,* July–August 2012 (accessed November 2, 2013).

13. www.brainyquote.com (accessed November 2, 2013).

Chapter 2

THE NEW HEALTHCARE MARKET

It is not the strongest of the species that survives, nor the most intelligent that survives. It is the one that is the most adaptable to change.

—Charles Darwin[1]

Imagine you're a sales representative selling a new medical device. You spend months working with a physician champion at a key customer. The physician is convinced of the potential benefits of your new solution, which has recently been approved for marketing. Before the physician champion is allowed to evaluate the new technology at the hospital, the hospital value analysis committee (VAC) has to review the technology. The physician puts you in touch with the director of materials management, who leads the VAC.

In order to get the technology in front of the committee, the materials management director asks you to complete a long application. You are asked to provide pages of details about the device, its costs, its benefits, pricing, expected utilization, and evidence to support its value. Basically, the hospital wants to know how the device will decrease costs, improve quality, or enhance outcomes. You're told that the VAC meeting is closed to suppliers and that you therefore can't attend.

The required forms are completed and submitted. It seems like weeks have passed when you finally hear back. The director of materials sends a curt email stating that the committee has decided that the device doesn't provide enough benefits to warrant an evaluation. Any hopes of getting it on contract are crushed.[2]

Welcome to the new buyer of healthcare. Although this is a simplified example and most experienced sales professionals could point out many problems with the sales approach described in the story, it's intended to make a point—the healthcare market is changing. This is particularly true for markets like the United States.

In the US, we now have healthcare reform, value-based purchasing, a maturing hospital supply chain, growing transparency on prices and quality, and a change in physician and hospital relationships. The net result is a focus on taking costs out and bringing quality into the buying decision.

The buying decision is changing. Therefore, companies that sell and market supplies and services to healthcare providers must also change. This is particularly true for companies that have been selling physician-preference items (PPIs). These are the items for which strong supplier relationships with the physician made it harder for hospital administration to attack the supply costs.

It's important to consider this changing environment, since it will have a big impact on selling in the future. Even more important is putting yourself in your customer's shoes to try to understand how their world is changing. Many of the drivers of change are impacting your customer in ways they may not yet fully understand.

Some of the topics in this chapter are a bit complex, but your ability to master these will help you be seen as a real resource for your customer, not just as someone trying to hit a sales quota. In this chapter, we discuss these drivers of change and the implications for your customer, and for selling and defending your value.

TEN DRIVERS OF CHANGE

In the "new normal" of healthcare buying, there are new influencers on the buying decision. It's not enough to merely sell the clinical features and benefits of a technology or solution to a physician or user. Now there are

VACs, technology assessment organizations, organizations looking at outcomes transparency, and new supply-chain disruptors.

In the United States and elsewhere, these changes are being driven by many factors, each of which is influencing the buying behavior of your customers. One of the critical common themes across all of the drivers is an increased focus on taking costs out and bringing quality in. Figure 2.1 provides an overview of the key drivers.

Figure 2.1. Ten drivers of change in healthcare

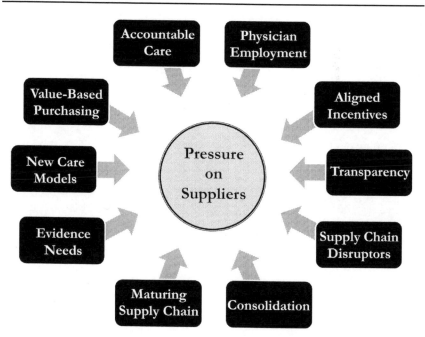

We'll explore each of these key drivers in detail. Some of these are the result of reimbursement changes. Since reimbursement is an evolving subject, we'll discuss the main concepts and ideas behind the reimbursement changes. You'll be provided links in the Notes section to locations to access up-to-date information.

Driving Force 1: Value-Based Purchasing

New reimbursement mechanisms encourage providers to deliver better outcomes and lower costs. This may sound strange, but in the US, the old reimbursement model paid for activity and costs. The more that an activity was done, and the more it cost, the more the provider was paid.

This fee-for-service model encouraged overuse of services, and waste. Some studies show an estimated $700+ billion in waste of all kinds in the US healthcare system.[3] This is changing. In the United States, for example, the Center for Medicare and Medicaid Services (CMS) has established new value-based purchasing incentives. Here is a high-level summary of these:

- *Reducing readmissions.* Under the old reimbursement model, providers were paid when a patient was readmitted for the same condition or diagnosis. For example, a patient who had surgery that was poorly done could be readmitted for follow-up care related to the poor surgical outcome. In essence, hospitals were paid for doing rework. The new reimbursement incentives penalize hospitals for excessive readmissions related to certain conditions.

- *Eliminating hospital acquired conditions (HACs).* HACs are conditions or events that occur while a patient is in the hospital. For example, if a patient was admitted for a simple surgical procedure and slipped and fell while in the hospital, the hospital was paid for treating the fall. Now, under value-based purchasing, hospitals are not paid for these HACs, or events that occur while in the hospital. Furthermore, future reimbursement mechanisms will penalize those hospitals that perform the worst.

- *Improving patient satisfaction.* Under value-based purchasing, hospitals are now measured on patient satisfaction. Hospitals that perform well relative to their peers or improve their performance over time receive financial incentives.

- *Improving process of care and outcomes.* Hospitals also have implemented specific measures regarding process of care and outcomes. In the US, CMS has tied financial incentives to these measures.

- *Reducing costs.* Hospitals in the US will have incentives in place to reduce total costs related to an inpatient stay over a 30-day period. This includes the cost of the inpatient event plus all outpatient follow-up costs for 30 days.

This is a high-level summary of the incentives and penalties in place for value-based purchasing. This summary is intentionally high-level, because the details of these incentives will likely change over time. Each year, CMS proposes and implements revisions to the rules. For more up-to-date or detailed information, please visit CMS.gov.

Driving Force 2: Accountable Care

Healthcare reform in the US brought with it accountable care organizations (ACOs) for Medicare beneficiaries. The ACO model has been piloted and used by private payers for some time.[4] Although there are different models for the Medicare ACO, the basic mechanics of ACOs are that networks of various healthcare providers care for a patient population over a period of three years.

The network can include physicians, hospitals, outpatient centers, laboratories, and others. Under the Medicare ACO models, there are incentives in place for the providers to reduce the total cost of care—both inpatient and outpatient care—for a patient during that period.

As the name implies, the idea is to make the providers "accountable" for the cost and quality of the care for these patients. There would be a disincentive for doing unnecessary procedures and tests. At the time of this writing, there are still questions about which of the ACO models will work and be in place in the future. However, the notion of CMS holding providers accountable for both inpatient costs and downstream costs of care probably won't go away.

Driving Force 3: Physician Employment Trends

In the US, some projections estimate that the share of physicians in private practice will be only 20 to 30 percent in the near future.[5] Of course, this employment percentage will vary by specialty and region. However, as physicians are increasingly employed by hospitals, their willingness to work more closely with hospitals on sourcing initiatives and consolidating suppliers increases. This change also means that suppliers who have relied almost exclusively on clinical relationships could be in danger.

Driving Force 4: Aligned Incentives

Closely connected to the physician employment trends is the idea of aligned incentives. Payers are becoming smarter about how they pay hospitals and physicians. In the United States, private payers and CMS have instituted or are piloting bundled payment programs. In the past, physicians and providers were paid separately for caring for a patient. Under the bundled payments program, there is one payment for caring for the patient over a specified period. The various stakeholders then decide how to split up that payment. Although there are different bundled payment models, the basic idea is to provide incentives to align the interest of the physician and hospital to take costs out and improve quality.

Driving Force 5: Transparency of Prices, Value, and Outcomes

The hospital supply chain has historically suffered from opaque pricing and relatively little comparative data on the value and outcomes of technologies and supplies. Think about yourself as a consumer. If you were purchasing a new television, you could turn to a number of potential sources for information on price, quality, and value. These range from formal services like *Consumer Reports* to peer-based reviews on websites like Amazon. The hospital supply market spends hundreds of billions of dollars with little comparative data.

There are generally three areas of transparency. One is price. This is simply the price for the device, drug, or supply item. Another is value. This means determining whether the supply item is a good value or which of the supply alternatives is the best value. The third area of transparency is outcomes. Outcomes are the short- and long-term outcomes associated with the technology or supply item. These include both clinical and economic outcomes.

Many researchers argue that this lack of transparency on price and quality had contributed to the increased costs of delivering healthcare. Many entities have recognized this and are actively working on ways to give providers access to transparency and information. The goal is to use information to help make better purchasing decisions that reduce costs, improve quality, and yield better long-term outcomes. Table 2.1 summarizes the entities providing transparency.

Table 2.1. Sources of Transparency

Type	Description	Examples
Outcomes	Provide transparency on longer-term cost and clinical outcomes of devices or drugs.	SharedClarity
Value	Provide tools and a platform to streamline value analysis, share value analyses, and improve sourcing.	ProcuredHealth
Price	Provide transparency on pricing data for supply items and services.	MDBuyline, Group Purchasing Organization (GPOs), and others

Driving Force 6: New Supply-Chain Disruptors

Group purchasing organizations (GPOs) have long been a part of the hospital supply chain. According to the Healthcare Supply Chain Association, GPOs date back to 1909, when the Hospital Superintendents of New York first considered establishing a purchasing agent for laundry services. In 1910 the first GPO, the Hospital Bureau of New York, was created. During the last quarter of the twentieth century, GPOs' importance grew as hospitals faced rising expenditures due to phenomenal advances in care and an aging population.[6]

The central role of GPOs had been to aggregate member purchasing in order to negotiate better terms with suppliers. Over time, GPOs added other supply-chain services such as benchmarking, consulting, and best practices. Traditionally, the aggregation approach worked well with supplies that were less differentiated, non clinician-preference items. For items that are physician-preference driven and for new technologies, GPOs have had far less success in leveraging buying power.[7] Let's face it—many hospitals have struggled with aligning their own physicians in order to standardize purchasing and save costs.

An entirely new set of start-ups have emerged to disrupt the old medical-technology sales model. These start-ups are focused on PPIs, supply items for which GPOs traditionally could not provide the same level of leverage as commodity items. PPIs can account for roughly 60 percent of supply costs. The new disruptors include companies like MedPassage, CurvoLabs, OrthoDirect, Corcardia, and ProcuredHealth.

These companies have different business models but largely the same broad objectives: taking costs out of and bringing quality into purchasing decisions. Such businesses are leveraging transparency and new business models to help providers achieve these objectives. Some are also providing alternative sales channels and models that are valuable for suppliers.

Driving Force 7: Hospital Consolidation and Aggregation

From 2007 to 2012, there were over 500 hospital acquisitions in the US.[8] Some predict that 20 percent of US hospitals will seek acquisition within the next five years.[9] Consolidation offers a number of benefits. It gives the hospitals efficiencies in operations and potentially provides leverage in negotiations with private payers. Consolidation also allows for potentially better coordination of care, which is becoming increasingly important under healthcare reform.

Consolidation usually confers a big supply-chain benefit, as well. The continued consolidation of the hospital market means that there will be mega-systems with enough buying power and leverage to take on supplier negotiations without the need of GPOs. Moreover, unlike most GPOs, these systems should be able to drive compliance with purchasing agreements and standardize purchasing within their organization. Studies have shown that GPO savings offered to their members tend to be uneven and to favor small to medium-sized hospitals.[10]

Hospitals have also historically had mixed feeling about the benefits of GPOs. Although many hospitals are actual GPO shareholders, they are not always satisfied with GPO performance. A recent survey by *Modern Healthcare* found that 84 percent of hospitals said that controlling prices paid for supplies was very important. Only 26 percent of the respondents were very satisfied with the performance of their GPO.[11] It is logical to assume that large systems have the ability to develop the expertise and processes to leverage their own purchasing power.

Many hospital systems are now coming together regionally to form new joint ventures to build critical mass in the market. These are not mergers, but rather the creation of new legal entities to enable collaboration. A key area of collaboration is in leveraging purchasing volume and creating best practice care pathways. These systems believe they can take substantial costs out by leveraging spend.[12]

Driving Force 8: Growing Importance of Hospital Supply Chains

In the United States alone, hospitals and other healthcare providers spend about $300 billion dollars annually on supplies and services to support care delivery.[13] These include pharmaceuticals, medical devices, diagnostics, support services, and capital purchases, and range from highly innovative imaging technologies to basic stethoscopes and bandages to janitorial services. It's an astonishing amount of spending. Figure 2.2 shows a typical view of hospital cost structure and supply spending.[14]

Figure 2.2. Hospital cost structure and supply costs

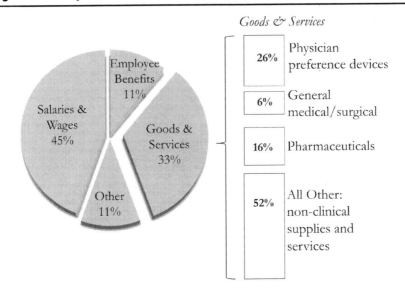

It is important to put this spend into perspective. In the US, supplies and services are estimated to account for approximately 30 to 40 percent of the cost of a procedure.[15] Supply costs are expected to grow at double the rate of other costs in the future in light of new technologies and continued hospital outsourcing.[16] For hospitals and other providers, containing the cost of supplies and services should be a critical activity.

Moreover, given the financial health of the hospital industry, it becomes even more evident that cost control and smart buying should be a critical competency. US hospitals, on average, operate on very thin profit margins. Over the past decade or so, operating margins—or revenue minus the cost of operations—have been in the low single digits.[17] Thus, managing suppliers and supplies should be a critical function for providers.

Given the amount of money being spent and the projected impact, it would be reasonable to assume that healthcare supply chains and purchasing are highly sophisticated buyers. However, the opposite is true. By many accounts, the provider supply chain and purchasing functions for healthcare lag far behind those for other industries.[18] The auto, electronics, and consumer packaged goods industries, for example, take a far more sophisticated approach to managing suppliers and to buying goods and services.

Of course, this is a broad generalization and is not true of every hospital or hospital system. For example, the University of Pittsburgh Medical Center (UPMC), a large hospital system in Pennsylvania, was rated one of the top twenty-five healthcare supply chains for the past couple of years.[19] This ranking includes all types of businesses in healthcare, from hospitals to manufacturers to distributors. This list includes a number of other well-known healthcare systems, such as the Mayo Foundation, Geisinger Healthsystem, and Intermountain Health. These institutions, however, are the exception, not the rule, in the hospital business.

If you sell to providers today, you may be dealing with some sophisticated supply-chain and materials-management people. You probably also have encountered VACs. These are cross-functional teams focused on making a balanced buying decision. However, in general, healthcare leadership is just now beginning to recognize that the supply chain and suppliers could be a big source of value.

A number of forces have allowed hospitals and providers to be unsophisticated buyers in the past. Many of these forces are changing quickly. The changes include new reimbursement models, reduced reimbursement rates, and physician employment trends. All of these are creating a new normal of buying behavior.

If you are a supplier or a sales professional selling to providers, why does this matter to you? Simple: as providers become smarter buyers of good and services, how they evaluate you as a supplier and salesperson will change dramatically. In addition, the people involved in the buying decision and their relative influence will change. Anyone who has been selling for a while surely recognizes the shift that is underway in the buying decision.

Driving Force 9: Growing Evidence Requirements

A long-term trend for many payers and providers has been the increasing need for evidence for buying decisions. This trend has been accelerating, as many providers are now faced with new reimbursement models that reward reduced costs and improved quality. The obvious question when comparing one supply item with another or a new technology with an old one is whether it is a good value for the money. Suppliers will need to not only quantify the value differences but also provide evidence to substantiate them.

Driving Force 10: New Business and Care Models

A business model simply describes how an organization creates, delivers, and captures value.[20] One of the more famous examples of a new business model is Amazon. Amazon initially changed how most consumers searched for and purchased books.

This new business model essentially wiped out most brick-and-mortar bookstores. Think about how many bookstores—large chains as well as local stores—have disappeared. Borders was a victim, in part, of the Amazon business model. Now Amazon is doing the same thing to other consumer markets, like electronics and household goods.

Will Amazon start selling angioplasties? Probably not. However, many other entities in healthcare are focused on delivering care that is better, cheaper, and more convenient for patients. This in turn could affect how suppliers think about selling value. One established example is MinuteClinic. MinuteClinic, a subsidiary of CVS Caremark Corporation, is the largest provider of retail health clinics in the United States, with a network of 650 clinics in 27 states.[21] They focus on common medical conditions such as strep throat, flu, and pregnancy testing.

While MinuteClinic may not be a big sales opportunity for most suppliers, other business models are emerging in different parts of healthcare delivery that could have an impact. An example of a disruptive service provider is WeCare TLC, a company that develops and manages worksite primary-care clinics for employers and manages specialty care for employers. WeCare TLC provides an integrated medical management platform, care processes and tools, and a clinic. Their model is proved to significantly reduce per-employee per-month healthcare costs. They also drive down costs for expensive services. For instance, in Indiana, WeCare

TLC negotiated a contract for $450 MRI exams in a market that had technical fees ranging between $1,750 and $3,200.[22]

As employers get smarter about managing healthcare costs for their employees, this will impact care models and patient flow. Walmart is a great example of this effect. In 2012, Walmart announced that covered employees and their families who needed heart surgery, transplant surgery, or spinal surgery would be able to receive care with no out-of-pocket costs at six prominent health systems around the country. This announcement followed similar moves by other large employers, including Lowe's.[23] Employers are beginning to recognize that quality care at such institutions actually lowers costs.

CHANGING BUYER SOPHISTICATION

All of the drivers mentioned above mean that the buying decision and process is changing. Furthermore, the buyer is becoming much more sophisticated. The old buying process, which was often driven by clinical relationships, is being replaced by a more sophisticated buyer. This doesn't mean that clinical influence will disappear. It means that buying decisions will be more balanced and will consider clinical and economic value.

In order to make this real, think about your customers. Figure 2.3 is a simple buyer maturity scale. It describes the maturity of the provider supply chain and purchasing. The first column is low skilled, the next is basic, and the final is transformational. Take a few minutes and estimate the percentages of your customers that would fall into each category today. If you've been selling for more than five years, think about what percentages of your customers would have been in each bucket five years ago.

This exercise has been done with many salespeople across various parts of the healthcare marketplace. Most suppliers say that the bulk of their customers are in the first two columns. Very few have any customers they would say are all the way to the right—transformational.

Figure 2.3. Material management maturity

Low	Material Management Maturity	High
Tactical	*Business Perspective*	Strategic
Get supplies in	*Focus*	Costs & Outcomes
Low	*Involvement in Buying Decisions*	High
Narrow	*Value Recognition*	Broader

Low Skill	Basic	Transformational
• Very price focused • Get supplies in • Don't recognize value	• Price & value focus • Growing influence • More sophisticated	• Beyond price savings only • Outcomes oriented • Suppliers as a capability

What does this have to do with selling value? Many forces are changing how your customer buys. These forces will rapidly shift the buying behavior of your customer and the sophistication of their supply chain. With this shift in buying behavior and sophistication will come very different expectations of you as a supplier.

Your customers will also become much tougher negotiators as the buying power shifts from purely clinical decisions to a balance of clinical and economic buying considerations. If you are in sales, you'll be expected to not just be able to sell the clinical value of your solution. You will also be expected to connect the economic value of your solution to a customer's business and business model.

This is the purpose and mission of this book. The goal is to help suppliers and their salespeople transition to selling their value in the new normal of healthcare.

ALIGN VALUE SELLING EFFORTS WITH THE NEW MARKET

Some would argue that all of these changes mean the end of the clinical salesperson. In other words, the economic buyers will hold all the power, and clinical selling will no longer be important. While this may be true for some clinical supply items, clinical selling will always be important for most items and services. This is particularly true for new technologies and situations that require supplier expertise and ongoing technical support.

However, the degree of influence of clinicians and users in the buying decision has diminished and will likely continue to diminish. One simple thing a supplier can do is compare its current sales focus with where its sales focus should be in the future based on the changes happening in the market.

If you are a salesperson, you can also do this exercise for your own territory. Figure 2.4 is an example of a simple exercise. Simply list the percentage of time and effort spent with each of these buying influences today. Next, think about where the effort *should* be today, and then where it should be in a few years.

In order to determine how much time you should spend on each buying influence, consider how they currently influence the purchase decision and how they will influence it in the future. In other words, how much of the buying decision can or does each buying influence have today and in the future? Obviously, this will vary by customer and segment. Therefore, you'll have to come up with a rough estimate.

If you're like most sales organizations and suppliers, your customers and the market are probably changing much faster than you are. Companies that sell clinically based products and that go through an exercise like this often find that they are overinvesting in efforts to sell clinically, and underinvesting in efforts to reach non-clinical buyers.

When you think about the future, it's important to consider both the outside and the inside. From an outside perspective, consider how customers will continue to evolve. Will they continue to consolidate? Will the financial pressures continue? Also, think about how competition might change over time. Will you face new competition from low-cost suppliers? These are all good questions to ask.

Figure 2.4. Buying influence assessment

Clinical	Finance	Supply Chain	Other
• Physicians	• CFO	• Materials Mgmt	• Risk Mgmt
• Nurses & Techs	• Director	• Strategic Sourcing	• Quality
• Department Heads	• Billing	• Logistics	• Lean
Current Influence on Buying Decision _(% of buying decision – Total 100%)_			
% of Time Spent with Each (Total 100%)			
Future Influence on Buying Decision _(% of buying decision – Total 100%)_			
% of Future Time Spent with Each (Total 100%)			

From an inside perspective, consider your current sales bag and your future portfolio. In general, as a product line matures, your customers will need less technical support and will be willing to assume more of the risks associated with switching suppliers. This means that the economic buyers will have more influence. The opposite is generally true as well. When product lines are new to the market, they require more technical support and service. This is when the users or clinicians have more influence.

If you evaluate this from a sales territory perspective and find that you're not spending enough time with non-clinical buyers, hopefully the content in the remaining parts of this book will provide the necessary insights. These, along with the tools and preparing, should get you ready to sell and defend your value.

KEY TAKEAWAYS

- Ten key factors are driving change in the healthcare market.

- Understanding these ten factors and how they impact your company, market, or sales territory is critical to preparing for future success.

- Hospitals are becoming more sophisticated as buyers. You need to match your value selling strategy to the buyer's level of sophistication.

- In light of the change in the marketplace, the people involved in the buying decision are shifting.

- You should evaluate where you spend your sales time today and compare it with where you *should* be spending your time based on the influence of various people involved.

NOTES

1. www.ThinkExist.com (accessed February 8, 2014).

2. This story was developed based on personal experience and the stories of many salespeople. The idea was derived from E. Anderson, "Death of a Medtech Salesman" [Blog], http://www. Biodesignalumni.doc, 2012 (accessed November 2, 2013).

3. Lallemand N. Cafarella, "Reducing Waste in Healthcare," Healthaffairs.org, December 13, 2012 (accessed November 2, 2013).

4. D. Muhlestein, *Continued Growth of Public and Private Accountable Care Organizations,* Healthaffairs.org, February 19, 2013 (accessed November 2, 2013).

5. The proportion of physicians employed by hospitals is increasing. There is some debate about the current percentage being employed and what the future will bring. This article provides some projections. D. Beaulieu, "Physician Employment Could Hit 75%, Eclipsing Private Practice," Fierceparacticemanagement.com, July 18, 2012 (accessed November 2, 2013).

6. R. Saha et al., "A Research Agenda for Emerging Roles of Healthcare GPOs and Their Evolution from Group Purchasing to Information Sharing to Strategic Consulting," in *Proceedings of the 43rd Hawaii International Conference on System Sciences,* 2010.

7. See GAO Report, *Group Purchasing Organizations: Use of Contracting Processes and Strategies to Award Contracts for Medical-Surgical Product,* July 16, 2003.

8. S. Kliff, "Hospital Chains Keep Getting Bigger," *Washington Post,* June 3, 2013 (accessed November 2, 2013).

9. J. Cresswell and R. Abelson, "New Laws and Rising Costs Create a Surge of Supersizing Hospitals," *New York Times,* August 12, 2013 (accessed November 2, 2013).

10. See GAO Report, "Group Purchasing Organizations."

11. J. Lee, "Supply Side Economics," *Modern Healthcare,* August 18, 2012 (accessed November 2, 2013).

12. L. Butcher, "Collaboration Equals Independence," *Hospital & Health Networks,* January 1, 2012 (accessed November 2, 2013).

13. M. Clapp, M. Rie, and P. Zweig, "How a Cabal Keeps Generics Scarce," *New York Times,* September 2, 2013 (accessed November 2, 2013).

14. Adapted from "The Benefits of a Successful Value Analysis Program" [Webcast], *WellStar*, www.iienet.org (accessed November 2, 2013).

15. K. Montgomery and E. Schneller, "Hospital Strategies for Orchestrating Selection of Physician Preference Items," *Milbank Quarterly*, 85.2 (2007).

16. Ibid.

17. American Hospital Association Chartbook, AHA.org (accessed November 2, 2013).

18. Montgomery and Schneller, "Hospital Strategies for Orchestrating Selection of Physician Preference Items."

19. "Gartner Announces Rankings of Its 2013 Healthcare Supply Chain Top 25," *Gartner*, www.Gartner.com, November 25, 2013 (accessed December 1, 2013).

20. See Wikipedia.org.

21. See www.minuteclinic.com.

22. B. Klepper, "Are You Ready for Intense Price Competition," *Brian Klepper Blog*, October 7, 2012 (accessed November 2, 2013).

23. J. Lee, "Lowes and Home Depot to Offer Employees a Leg Up on Knee and Hip Work at Certain Systems," *Modern Healthcare*, October 8, 2013 (accessed November 2, 2013).

PART II

UNDERSTAND THE NEW BUYER

MAP THE BUYING PROCESS AND CENTER

All business success rests on something labeled a sale, which at least momentarily weds company and customer.

—Tom Peters, management guru[1]

All of the changes happening to healthcare are having a big impact on customers. One of the biggest areas of impact is the buying process and buying center. The term "buying process" just means how the customer buys goods and services. "Buying center" refers to who is involved in the buying process and what role they play in the purchasing decision.

For suppliers, these are critical areas to understand. An analogy might help explain the importance of understanding these two areas. Picture a pilot flying a plane in clear blue skies. The pilot's ability to see where he's going and what's around him makes flying relatively easy. In the United States, this is called visual flight rules (VFR) flying. Pilots flying under VFR assume responsibility for their separation from all other aircraft and are generally not assigned routes or altitudes by air traffic control.[2]

When the weather makes visual flying difficult or impossible, pilots must use their instrumentation to safely navigate and fly the plane. This is called instrument flight rules (IFR). These cloudy skies require a different level of skills, training, and special certification. The conditions also require a different set of tools to safely fly.

What does this have to do with the buying process? If you've been selling to an account for many years, you probably clearly understand their buying process and key decision makers. You most likely have also built good relationships with the key decision makers and influencers. This is like flying in clear skies. Things are relatively clear and easy.

What happens when the account's situation changes dramatically? Maybe there's a new VP of Supply Chain who changes all the rules governing how the hospital will buy. Alternatively, you could be given a new, complex account. In this situation, you may need a structured approach to understanding the buying process and buying center.

As professional buyers assume a more critical role in the buying process at many of your customers, your ability to sell in cloudy skies becomes even more important. This is because professional buyers have at their disposal an entire set of tricks and tactics to cloud the buying process. They often act like they are the decision maker when in fact they are not. So your ability to sell in "cloudy skies" will become even more important as your customers become more sophisticated at buying.

Understanding the buying dynamics is a critical step in ensuring that you are paid fairly for the value your solutions bring to customers. There are two key steps to understanding the buying dynamic that I discuss in this chapter. First, I review a process for mapping who is involved in the buying decision and their role in the buying process. Next, I reveal a standard hospital-buying process and provide insights on how to engage strategically during this process.

EXAMPLE OF PURCHASING GAMES

A story will help illustrate this change happening in the buying process. The names have been disguised, but the story is real, told by many salespeople.

Joe is a seasoned business development executive. He had been calling on his customer for about eight years. Six years ago, the customer purchased new equipment from Joe's company. Five months ago, the customer went through an update cycle, replacing that equipment with new equipment to support their expanding operation.

The equipment Joe sells is a critical component of the customer's operations. In fact, not long after the customer installed and went live with

Joe's equipment six years ago, the customer told Joe how much more efficient and durable Joe's equipment was than the previous equipment. It needed fewer repairs, required less maintenance, and suffered almost no downtime during critical operations. The department head even went so far as to explain how much money Joe's solution saved the company.

Until recently, Joe had dealt almost entirely with the technical staff and department head at this customer. Since the type of capital equipment he sells needs some configuration to fit into a customer's operations, the customer's technical staff had been the key decision maker in the buying process.

Because this was a capital purchase, ultimately the CFO of the account signed off on the purchase. However, in the past, if capital was available and the equipment needed upgrading, the department head and technical staff usually drove the buying process and made the decisions. This is because the technical staff would be stuck with any problems that arose in the selection and installation of equipment.

Joe had built strong relationships with the equipment users and technical staff over the years. This time, however, things were different. Out of the blue, Joe received a request for proposal (RFP) from the customer's purchasing function. He called his key technical contacts at the customer to find out what was going on. They told him, "Sorry, we have a new purchasing policy we have to follow." His contacts said that talking to Joe during the RFP process would violate their new bidding rules.

Joe decided to set up a meeting with purchasing to better understand the new RFP process and get more background for the bid. He explained to the buyer in materials management that he just wanted to make sure he was following their new process. She reluctantly agreed to meet with him. He scheduled an hour-long meeting for 10 a.m. the following day.

On the day of the meeting, Joe arrived 20 minutes early. He reviewed his objectives for the meeting, the key questions he had developed, and his notes. He was eager to make a good impression. He was confident in the value that his company had brought to this customer, but nervous about the new RFP process. He was to meet with Andrea, the lead buyer for the equipment. At 10 a.m. he was ushered into a small conference room. He was told that Andrea would be along shortly. It was a small, cramped, dimly lit room with a bit of a musty odor. It reminded Joe of the police interrogation rooms he had seen on TV.

At 10:35, Andrea arrived in the meeting room. She introduced herself and apologized for the delay. She appeared professional and cordial. Joe tried to engage her in small talk and build rapport, but she avoided engaging. She said she only had 20 minutes and wanted to get to the point.

In her opinion, Joe's company had been taking advantage of them. She believed that Joe's company had been overcharging for equipment as well as annual service contracts. She had purchased similar equipment at another hospital and knew that Joe's prices were "outrageous."

Joe tried to explain the differences between his solution and others. Andrea responded, "All the solutions are the same—it's going to come down to price." Joe tried to provide her some of the feedback on the savings that his solution had provided. She said that that was six years ago, and that these types of solutions were now a commodity.

She told Joe that he was one of four competitors, all of whom offered good solutions. The bid would come down to price. As Joe attempted to provide more background, she stopped him in midsentence and ended the meeting. She needed to meet with one of his competitors to discuss their bid.

The customer engaged in multiple RFP rounds. They called it "down-selecting." First, there were four bidders. The buyer screened out two of the suppliers. The buyer then announced that they wanted the "best and final" bid. Ultimately, Joe retained the business at much lower margins. Moreover, he felt confused and abused as a result of the RFP experience. The eight years of investing in relationships with the customer seemed to have been a waste.

This story illustrates the challenges of selling in a changing world where professional buyers are involved. As these buyers play an increasingly important role in the buying process, it becomes critical that your selling process changes. Professional buyers employ a range of strategic sourcing and negotiation tactics that are meant to extract value from suppliers. Understanding their tactics, process, and interests in the context of the broader organization will help you capture the value you deserve.

UNDERSTAND THE BUYING PROCESS

Most organizations follow a process for buying goods and services. Some hospitals may use a very formal process. There may be strict rules about how the process works, who needs to be involved, and how decisions will be made. Others may be less formal. Also, the type of supply item they buy may influence the formality of their process. In some countries or regions of the world, regulations govern the process providers must follow in order to buy new good or services. However, as a general rule, most organizations follow a process comprising clear buying stages.[3]

Figure 3.1. Buying process overview

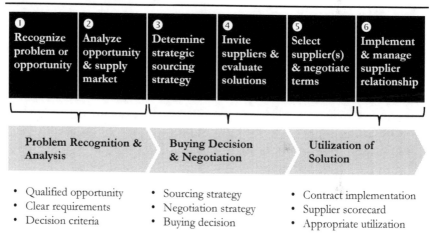

| ❶ Recognize problem or opportunity | ❷ Analyze opportunity & supply market | ❸ Determine strategic sourcing strategy | ❹ Invite suppliers & evaluate solutions | ❺ Select supplier(s) & negotiate terms | ❻ Implement & manage supplier relationship |

Problem Recognition & Analysis	Buying Decision & Negotiation	Utilization of Solution
• Qualified opportunity • Clear requirements • Decision criteria	• Sourcing strategy • Negotiation strategy • Buying decision	• Contract implementation • Supplier scorecard • Appropriate utilization

Figure 3.1 shows a standard buying process. There are six buying stages. As a supplier, it's important to understand each of the stages and what the buyer is trying to accomplish at each stage. Moreover, it's important to understand that if you're not engaged early in the process, you lose a potential opportunity to educate the buyer and shape the buying decision.

Stage 1—Problem or Opportunity Recognition

This is when the customer recognizes that there is a problem or an opportunity that a supplier could help with. This recognition can come from many places. Depending on the skills of the supply chain organization, the problem or opportunity recognition could be driven by professional buyers. In fact, as customers become more sophisticated buyers, the opportunity recognition is often driven by purchasing or procurement. In general, the following are ways the customer recognizes there's a problem or an opportunity:

- *Suppliers.* Suppliers can be a valuable source of ideas to help the customer find new opportunities to reduce costs, improve productivity, grow revenue, improve outcomes, or minimize risk.

- *Benchmarking.* Customers can benchmark with other hospitals or providers to identify new opportunities. These benchmarks could be purchasing strategies, price benchmarks for supply items, cost benchmarking, and outcomes and quality benchmarks. Many hospitals belong to formal services that provide benchmarking of supply quality and prices. Group purchasing organizations (GPOs) and regional buying groups can also be a source of benchmark information.

- *Consultants.* Consultants are often a good source of new ideas and opportunities to reduce costs and improve performance. Purchasing consultants, in particular, give customers new ideas for reducing supply costs or getting more value from suppliers.

- *Conferences.* Providers often attend conferences to learn new ways of managing supply costs, improving quality and outcomes, and evolving their business model.

- *Customer's own data.* Customers regularly review financial and operational performance. This can lead them to recognize a problem or an opportunity.

Stage 2—Analyze Opportunity and Supply Market

At this stage, the customer's first goal is to confirm that the opportunity exists and to quantify it. This can be done with or without supplier assistance. For example, you may be the primary vendor for a particular supply item. The customer may have attended a conference and learned that many of their peers are paying much less for the items you sell. This apparent overpaying for a supply item will lead the customer to perform some analysis. The buyer will want to understand what kind of savings possibilities exist by reducing the price of the supply item.

Next, the customer will want to assess the supply market and their own buying patterns. They will try to answer the following questions:

- How much is spent on this good or service?

- Is spending going up or declining?

- What suppliers provide this good or service?

- What are the suppliers' reputations, and how well do they perform?

- What are the strengths and weaknesses of suppliers?

- Are there many suppliers, or few, for this category?

- How important is this supply item to the business?

- How quickly does technology change?

- Who are the users, and what is their level of support for change?

After this stage the customer should have a good idea of whether an opportunity exists. They should also have some insights that will help them formulate a sourcing strategy for the supply item.

Stage 3—Determine Strategic Sourcing Strategy

Based on the analysis done in Stage 2, the customer will formulate a sourcing strategy. We'll talk a lot more about the sourcing strategies buyers use. However, at a basic level, it is the customer's strategy for buying a good or service.

For example, you may sell a supply item that represents a small portion of the customer's supply costs. The customer may decide to save time by doing a simple RFP. Alternatively, the customer may simply turn to their GPO contract for the supply item. We'll discuss all of the various sourcing strategies in the next chapter.

Stage 4—Invite Suppliers and Evaluate Solutions

The sourcing strategy will determine how the customer engages suppliers. A supply category that is less differentiated, with many potential suppliers, may result in an RFP or a reverse auction. On the other hand, for a highly specialized supply item there may be only one potential supplier. So, which suppliers are invited and how the customer evaluates solutions will vary widely depending on the characteristics of the supply market and the customer's buying history.

The Corporate Executive Board estimates that 57 percent of the buying decision is made by the time the customer contacts suppliers.[4] Once you understand the buying process, it should be clear why this is the case. Buying stages 1 through 3 can sometimes be completed without contacting suppliers.

For example, a purchasing agent may learn that other customers are paying less for what you supply. The purchasing agent could do some benchmarking and analysis. This might lead the customer to develop a strategy to send the item you sell out to bid through an RFP. If you are the incumbent and receive a "surprise" RFP, it could simply mean that the buyer is playing a game to try to get you to lower your price.

At this stage of the buying process, if this were a serious sourcing initiative, the buyer would be evaluating the suppliers' capabilities as well as their solutions. Supplier capabilities are the people, process, expertise, and technology that the supplier brings in addition to a specific product or service. This includes things like supply chain capability, special services, and the supplier's research and development.

A simple way to determine whether the buyer is playing games with you is to see what kind of evaluation of the various suppliers' solutions is being conducted. If you are on the outside and invited to bid, you should ask the buyer how the evaluation will be conducted. If they are not going to do a real evaluation, it's probably not a serious bid request.

Stage 5—Select Suppliers and Negotiate Terms

If you've made it this far, it's a good sign. At this stage, the buyer selects the supplier or suppliers. Depending on the supply item, the buyer may use different strategies for buying and for managing suppliers. For example, the supply item could be a critical item for which the buyer wants to have more than one supplier. The buyer may be concerned that a supply disruption will create a serious issue for the hospital. In this case, they may use a dual sourcing strategy.

Moreover, it could be that the technology in a given supply category changes rapidly and that the buyer wants to have multiple suppliers on contract in order to have access to their future innovations. In this case, the buyer might choose two suppliers. Sometimes one supplier is the primary vendor and the other is secondary. This arrangement gives the buyer relationships with both suppliers and access to new technologies as things change.

At this stage, the buyer also negotiates final terms. This can be a great opportunity for the buyer to extract more value from you. Since you've made it this far, you may not be as concerned with some of the final details of the deal. This is what clever buyers are looking for. They know that you are under pressure to get the deal signed. They can use this as an opportunity to "nibble" away at your value. This comes in the form of asking for extra service, special deliveries, different payment terms, and other seemingly non-core parts of the deal. I talk in later chapters about how to deal with this nibbling-away of value.

Stage 6—Implement Agreement and Manage Supplier Relationships

Smart buyers realize that an agreement is only a piece of paper. Any savings or value that emerges from a relationship with a supplier comes from implementing the agreement and from the ongoing managing of the relationship. Just as sellers have a process called customer relationship management, buyers have a similar process called supplier relationship management (SRM). SRM is a process of maximizing the value of the relationship with a critical subset of suppliers who can help the customer achieve its strategic objectives.

At this stage of the buying process, it may be tempting to simply get the sale and move on. However, closely managing the relationship through regular business reviews can offer a big opportunity to make the buyer truly understand the value you bring as a supplier. The SRM process typically focuses on the following:[5]

- *Supplier performance evaluation.* This includes things such as on-time delivery, quality, and training and support. Many of these can be measured and put into a scorecard by the buyer. Depending on what you sell, this may be a great opportunity for you to put together a scorecard to remind the buyer of the value you bring. Buyers have short memories. If you wait until the next contract renewal to do this, you could miss an opportunity.

- *Idea and innovation sourcing.* Sophisticated buyers are interested in new ideas and innovations. They know that suppliers can be a great source of ideas. These ideas and innovations are not just products. They can be related to processes, best practices, and business models.

- *Joint cost reductions.* This may sound scary. However, you shouldn't assume that a joint cost-reduction effort is only focused on reducing your price. You may have, for example, process improvement experts who can work with the customer on process redesign to take costs out. On the other hand, there may be different ways to serve the customer that allow you to reduce your costs and pass those savings on to the customer.

The buying process will vary depending on the sophistication of the supply chain organization, the buying behavior of the customer's organization, the level of person you're engaged with, the customer's situation, and what you sell. However, understanding the generic buying process outlined here should give you good insights for identifying new opportunities to sell value.

In the story earlier in this chapter about the buying games, things seemed very confusing for the seller. If you view the situation with an understanding of the customer's buying process, it should be clearer what was going on. By the time the seller received the RFP, the customer had already gone through stages 1 through 3 of the buying process.

The seller didn't know whether this was a purchasing bluff or whether it was a serious bid. With an understanding of the buying process, he could have asked the right questions to better understand the situation. This could have helped him prepare a strategy to better defend his value.

Use Buying Process Strategically

Consider your own sales process. Take a moment and think about when in the customer's buying process you typically engage. Also, think about when the customer typically engages you. Is it at the beginning of their buying process, when they identify the problem or opportunity? Or is it at Stage 4, when they have already done much of the research and analysis?

Part of the answer may depend on what you sell. It can also depend on whether you are the primary vendor or are on the outside. However, regardless of your situation, understanding the customer buying process should help you be strategic about how you engage with customers.

Let's use an example. Assume that you have little or no relationship with a customer. Next, assume the customer contacts you and invites you to be part of an RFP. This may be flattering, and many people may get excited about the possibility of a potential new sale. An understanding of the buying process should lead you to ask some good questions before you invest your precious time and resources in responding to the bid.

In this example, the buyer may have no intention whatsoever of doing business with you. They could just be using you to try to get their incumbent's price down. They hope that you bid low so that they can use this low bid as leverage with their incumbent. Alternatively, it could be that the customer must gather three bids for any purchases above a certain dollar amount. In this case, they just need you to bid and do not intend to do business with you.

If you have little or no relationship with the account and are asked to bid without any real contact with them, you should ask some basic questions:

- Why did they contact your company?

- What problems are they trying to solve, or what issues do they have?

- What are their goals with this sourcing project?

- How will the decision be made? Are there fixed criteria established (e.g., price, quality, service, supply reliability)?

- Who is the current incumbent vendor?

- What's currently working well or not working well with their existing suppliers?

- Who are the key users or decision makers?

- Can you meet with the users or decision makers?

- If this is product related, can you do an evaluation with the key users or deciders?

Switching suppliers can be difficult for buyers. This is true for even simple supply items. If the customer has little or no experience with your company or solutions, then they will want to perform a thorough evaluation of your capabilities and solution before switching. Therefore, one simple way to gauge their seriousness is to test whether they will give you access to the key users and whether they will evaluate your solution. If they are not willing to do this, they are probably not serious about you as a supplier.

ASSESS THE BUYING CENTER

With the rise of the professional buyer comes a change in how customers buy things. The buying process, the people involved, and the criteria used often change as a customer becomes a more sophisticated buyer. This calls for a more sophisticated approach to selling and defending value. As the story in the beginning of the chapter shows, the buying process can change. When it does, you must adapt your selling approach or face significant pressure. One key step is to understand the buying center.

The buying center is simply the group of people involved in the purchasing decision. Sometimes this group is called the purchasing committee, the value analysis committee, or the decision-making unit. Regardless of its name, the concept is simple. There are people and groups involved in the buying decision. Each person or group can play a different role or multiple roles. It's important to understand who will be involved, what their role is, and their relative influence in the decision process.

Long ago, scholars studied how buying decisions get made in organizations. The result was the term "buying center." A helpful way to analyze the buying center is to break it into the following categories:[6]

- *User buyer:* the person or group who uses your product or service.

- *Gatekeeper:* the person or group who controls access to the customer and flow of information.

- *Purchaser:* the person or group who manages the buying process.

- *Influencer:* the person or group who influences the buying decision and supplier selection.

- *Decider:* the person or group who ultimately makes the buying decision.

- *Coach:* the person within the customer's organization who wants your solutions and guides you in the process.

Each of the above roles can be fulfilled by one person or by a group of people. In addition, one person or a group can play multiple roles. Many professional buyers are trained and learn to act like they are the decider. Unsuspecting salespeople can fall victim to this tactic.

Sometimes a professional buyer is given the authority to be the decider. This is rare. Buyers know that even deciding simple things like what office-supply vendor to standardize on can bring about complaints from within their organization. Smart professional buyers involve the users as a way to get buy-in and to manage the risk of something going wrong.

This shared responsibility does not prevent a professional buyer from *acting* like the decider. They know that pretending to be the decider often works. I once presented to a room of about a hundred professional buyers. When I asked them to raise their hands if they had ever pretended to be the decider when they weren't, most did so. Many were smiling. Professional buyers usually act as both purchaser and gatekeeper. They can also be an influencer, depending on the buying situation and procurement's maturity. However, they are rarely the sole decider.

MAP THE BUYING CENTER

A helpful exercise to get at the heart of the buying decision is to map the buying center. This entails simply determining who will be involved in the buying decision, their role, and who else might influence them. This exercise should be done early in the sales process and be updated as you gather more information. An example of the map for selling a new laboratory solution to a hospital is presented in Table 3.1.

Having a solid understanding of the buying center will help you cut through the noise and clouds that are often generated by professional buyers. Their goal is to de-value your offering, create leverage against you, and confuse you during the negotiation. The more they can do this, the greater their leverage. They're not evil; they're simply doing their job—trying to get a great deal for their business.

Mapping the account and clarifying how the decision will be made and who has influence is one of the key tools for preventing a disaster. Invoking the flying analogy again, these tools will help you when things get cloudy. Using the map below, you can clarify who the actual decider is, who influences whom in the buying process, and whether the buying center members are your company's friends or foes. You can also use this map to develop an account coverage strategy.

Table 3.1. Example of Buying Center Map

Buying center member	Who?	Relative influence? (1 = very little; 7 = very high)	Who influences them?	Friend or foe?
User buyer (uses your product or service)	Laboratory technicians	4	Director of laboratory	Mixed
Gatekeeper (controls access to customer and flow of information)	Hospital purchasing	2	Director of laboratory	Neutral
Purchaser (manages buying process)	Hospital purchasing	2	Director of laboratory	Neutral
Influencer (influences buying decision and supplier selection)	Dr. Smith, Pathologist	6	Director of laboratory	Moderate supporter
Decider (ultimately makes buying decision)	Laboratory value analysis committee	7		Neutral to moderate supporter
Coach (internal, wants your solutions and guides you in the process)	Laboratory manager	5		Strong supporter

EVALUATE PHYSICIAN ENGAGEMENT

Switching suppliers is not easy. Even for relatively simple supply items like office supplies, changing suppliers can create headaches for the supply chain organization. And for more clinically driven, physician-preference items, it can be even more difficult to switch suppliers. Therefore, engaging the physicians in the sourcing process is critical for the hospital purchasing department. For a supplier, this is one of the "clues" to how serious the customer is about switching suppliers.

If physicians are the users of the supply item you sell, it will be important to assess physician engagement with the hospital's sourcing effort. One of the historic challenges providers have faced, particularly in the US, is aligning physicians' interests with the interests of the hospital. This is particularly true for supply items that are high physician-preference items.

Figure 3.2. Assessing physician engagement in buying

Low	Physician Engagement in Buying	High
Low/No	**Moderate**	**High**
• Physicians not aware of contracting	• Physicians aware of contracting activities	• Physicians deliver negotiation points to suppliers
• Contracting done without physicians	• Some physicians engaged in sourcing process	• Physicians physically present for negotiations
• Physicians have negative view of purchasing	• Physicians in communication loop on negotiations	• Physicians know products' relative pricing
• No incentives in place to engage physicians		• Incentives in place

As you evaluate the buying center, it's important to understand the level of physician engagement with the sourcing efforts. Understanding the physicians' view of purchasing is also key. This holds true as well for non-physician users of technologies and services, such as laboratory technicians.

Watching for the level of engagement will give you clues about your progress in the sales and negotiation process. For example, materials management or the supply chain may tell you that the physicians are completely on board and willing to switch suppliers. This may or may not be accurate. You need to look for a few clues. Figure 3.2 summarizes these.[7]

Once you have a good sense of the level of physician engagement, you can better determine whether the sourcing initiative is for real. You can also use Table 3.1 to identify the specific level of engagement of key physician influencers in the account. It may be that some physicians are engaged, but not the right ones. Understanding this up front will help you during the negotiation stage.

CREATE LEVERAGE IN THE BUYING CENTER

One of the things that undermines a professional buyer's negotiation leverage is the interaction between the supplier and people within the customer organization. The goal of the professional buyer or lead negotiator at the customer is to create leverage. This leverage is usually created by qualifying as many suppliers as possible. The playing-off of one supplier against another is a simple negotiation tactic.

Smart buyers have learned that their own internal organization can be the biggest culprit in undermining the leverage they are trying to develop with suppliers. This is why they often create a formal set of rules for sourcing. These include eliminating contact with suppliers during the bid process, implementing formal information-sharing rules, and other tactics. Their goal is to undermine any leverage the seller might have, and to prevent "back door" selling.

Every connecting point between your company and the customer is a potential source of leverage. Each of the people in the customer account is a potential influencer who can help you. In general, there are a number of ways to create leverage with the buying center:

1. *Technical specifications.* Purchasing is usually the recipient of, but not the ones developing, the technical specifications. Working with key

users and influencers to determine or shape technical specifications can help ensure that you're in the driver's seat. It's not uncommon for tender or RFP specifications to emerge that essentially rule out all but one supplier based on technical specifications. If you're able to help set these, you will have an advantage.

2. *Evaluation criteria and weightings.* Many buying organizations put together evaluation criteria and weightings to help them make an "objective" decision about which supplier to select. I say more about this in later chapters. However, the criteria can include things like quality, service, price, delivery, and value-added services. Usually a weighting or scoring accompanies each factor. If you can shape or influence these criteria and weightings, you'll gain some leverage.

3. *Services as leverage.* When the product you are selling becomes less differentiated, the areas of leverage can then move to services. You should review all services that you provide to the account. Identify what services, whether free or charged, are provided. Determine whether these services are unique or differentiated from what competitors could provide. These could be areas like training, reimbursement services, and supply-chain and inventory services. Once you identify the services, see who in the account receives them. These could be important influencers you can leverage.

4. *Collaborations.* Many suppliers collaborate with customers in a number of ways, for example in new product development, research, or health policy advocacy. These collaborations typically involve people in the customer's business who have lots of influence. These can be potential people to leverage.

5. *Future technologies.* Many healthcare suppliers are fortunate to have a rich pipeline of new products. For many hospitals, new technologies allow them to better compete in their local communities and marketplace. At the same time, when a new technology is launched, suppliers often must choose which accounts get access to the technology, and in what order. Often,

it's just not feasible to service all customers who want a new technology right at launch. So, access to new technologies can be a source of leverage with some members of the buying center. Perhaps a purchasing agent won't care about it, but the hospital CFO may.

In the end, influencers come in many types and at many levels. A story conveyed by the VP of Supply Chain at a large hospital system may help illustrate this. His hospital system was conducting a strategic sourcing initiative for bagels. Yes, bagels. The hospital system had many hospitals across a region of the US. It had identified that it used many different suppliers for bagels. This is one of the signs of a potential savings opportunity for purchasing. That they had many different suppliers for the same supply item meant that standardizing on one supplier could drive some cost savings.

In this case, the bid process included a small local supplier and two national bagel companies. The buyer responsible for the sourcing initiative eliminated the local supplier and decided to standardize on one of the larger national suppliers because of the supplier's size and reach—a perfectly logical and by-the-book sourcing approach.

What the buyer didn't know was that the small local supplier had been serving bagels to many people in the main hospital for many years, including some who were now senior executives in the hospital system. The small local supplier was surprised to learn that it had been eliminated from the bid process. It used its relationships with the senior executives to pressure the buyers.

So, if a company selling bagels can use people in the account to create influence, so can you. It's not clear whether the small bagel company was successful or not in the end. However, this doesn't detract from the fact that they were able to persuade senior executives in the account to at least ask the buyer why the small supplier was shut out.

KEY TAKEAWAYS

- Almost 60 percent of the buying decision is made by the time the customer engages the supplier.

- Earlier in the buying process, the customer recognizes there's a problem or opportunity that a supplier can help with.

- If you are not working with the customer earlier in the buying process, you are missing an opportunity to shape the buying decision.

- Suppliers should understand the customer buying process and use this understanding strategically to sell and defend their value.

- Understanding the buying center is becoming more important as decisions shift from clinical buyers to more sophisticated professional buyers.

- Professional buyers are trained or learn to act like the decider in many buying situations. It is rarely the case, however, that the professional buyer is the sole decider.

- Mapping the buying center will give you a sense of who the real decider is along with the major influencers. With this information, you should have a plan for reaching the major influencers.

NOTES

1. www.brainyquote.com (accessed February 7, 2014).

2. See Wikipedia.org.

3. This buying process was developed based on the author's personal procurement experience. It was validated and refined through analysis of buying processes including University of Pittsburgh Medical Center (UPMC), www.UPMC.com/about/partners/supplychain (accessed November 2, 2013).

4. B. Adamson, M. Dixon, and N. Toman, "The End of Solution Selling," *Harvard Business Review*, HBR.org, July–August 2012 (accessed November 2, 2013).

5. C. Dominick and S. Lunney, *The Procurement Game Plan* (J. Ross Publishing, 2012).

6. Adapted from T. V. Bonoma, "Major Sales: Who Really Does the Buying?," *Harvard Business Review*, 1982, 111–19.

7. Adapted from E. Pursell, "Sourcing Physician Preference Supplies," Physician Preference Item Management Conference, March 18, 2008, ASU.Edu (accessed November 2, 2013).

Chapter | 4

ANTICIPATE BUYER SOURCING TACTICS

A good hockey player plays where the puck is. A great hockey player plays where the puck is going to be.

—Wayne Gretzky[1]

One of the principles we discussed in the introduction was trying to understand the perspective of the other side—your customer. Put yourself in the shoes of the VP of Supply Chain at a large health system. She has to buy tens of thousands of supply items to keep the hospital running. Each of these supply categories has a different supply dynamics and relative importance to the hospital's operation.

At this health system, there are also different users who wield widely varying influence on the buying decision. The goods and services purchased range from janitorial supplies to bagels to multi-million-dollar, high-tech imaging machines. Buying basic commodities requires a different level of user engagement than buying a highly advanced implantable medical device. Thus, the supply chain executive has to be smart about how to engage the users and gain buy-in.

At the same time, this VP of Supply Chain has a set of aggressive goals. She must drive costs out of the supply base each year. She is also responsible for evaluating new technologies and keeping physicians happy. Finally, she has to ensure high-quality sources of supplies and services, with no disruption. It's not an easy job.

Smart supply-chain leaders at hospitals have realized that they need to approach the sourcing of goods and services in a strategic way. Supply costs represent 30 to 40% of the total procedure cost.[2] Many projections have supply costs increasing as a percentage of overall hospital costs as new technologies continue to be released and as hospitals outsource more functions in the future.

Furthermore, many hospitals are now beginning to recognize the importance of the supply chain in creating value for the hospital. By many accounts, the hospital industry as a whole has a poorly run supply chain compared with other industries.[3] This is not to say that all hospital supply chains are poorly run. There are certainly many high-performing hospital supply chains. However, as an industry, there is much room for improvement. And as hospital supply chains improve, suppliers should expect much more pressure.

This chapter provides a window into how professional buying organizations source goods and services. With a better understanding of the sourcing process, sourcing strategies, and how professional buyers think, you will be better prepared to sell and defend your value. You need to anticipate where the buyer is going to be if you are to have the best possible chance at selling and defending your value.

STRATEGIC SOURCING

Strategic sourcing is a process for extracting more value from the supplier network. This doesn't always mean that it is focused on getting the lowest price. It also doesn't mean that it is about always buying from the best-quality supplier. It means finding the right supplier for the particular good or service being sourced.[4] It is also supposed to be aligned with the hospital's overall strategy and goals.

In many industries, the strategic sourcing for a particular category of supply items is led by an expert in that area. Often this is someone who actually knows much more about the market and the supply items than the salesperson from the supplier who is trying to sell to him or her. In most hospitals, that level of expertise in various supply categories does not yet exist. Given the complexity of the hospital supply chain, it's not clear that hospitals could develop this level of sophistication. However, buyers in general will become much more sophisticated over time.

Strategic sourcing is a process. If you are a supplier who has to engage in this process, it is helpful to understand what the buyers are trying to accomplish. Some buyers will be open and honest about their sourcing process and their goals. Others will try to play games. In general, any strategic sourcing process is intended to achieve some broad goals or "jobs." For a hospital, these goals or "jobs" are the following:

- *Align with hospital goals.* The sourcing process should align with the hospital's goals and objectives. Look carefully for any apparent mismatch between the hospital's overall goals and how a specific sourcing initiative is being conducted. For example, if a hospital is focused on becoming a center of excellence and the buying process seems to be all about price, this could signal that there is an issue. It is possible that the buyer is playing a game with you. Alternatively, it could be that you're dealing with a junior buyer who is not sourcing the supply items in the right way. In either case, you should ask questions and call out the apparent mismatch.

- *Reduce costs.* Let's be honest. The primary driver for many strategic sourcing initiatives in the past was to reduce costs. Hospitals operate on thin margins, and are always under pressure to take costs out. If you look at any survey of hospital executives, reducing costs is always their number one or number two goal.[5] The reduction in costs could be through price reductions, reductions in other costs within the hospital, or in cost reductions downstream, outside of the acute care setting. Under healthcare reform, suppliers with a good value story that addresses taking costs out both within the hospital setting and downstream will have an advantage.

- *Improve outcomes and quality.* Improving outcomes, quality, and patient satisfaction is a critical focus of most hospitals. This is partially driven by the payment and reimbursement reforms being implemented. The hospital supply chain is now looking to play a leadership role in evaluating costs, quality, and outcomes.[6] Suppliers who are prepared to connect the dots for the customer by showing how their solution impacts outcomes, quality, or satisfaction will be winners.

- *Improve reimbursement.* Healthcare reform in the US has brought in many new incentives and penalties to encourage providers to improve the quality of care and patient satisfaction. Smart suppliers who have an advantage in helping the customer in any of these areas should be prepared to highlight these advantages.

- *Manage supply risk.* Smart buyers have learned through painful experience that many suppliers experience quality issues and supply disruption. Managing supply risk has become even more important for many buyers as supply chains have become global. Managing supply risk is usually a key component of any buying criteria for professional buyers.

- *Gain access to innovation and ideas.* More sophisticated buyers understand that suppliers can be a great source of innovation and ideas. Innovation isn't just products. It can include process or business model innovation. If you are a supplier with a robust pipeline of innovations, you should think about how to use this strategically in selling and managing customers.

- *Improve service.* Improving service can be thought of broadly. This can include things like delivery, support, training, and value-added programs. It can also include things like improving safety.

- *Enhance social responsibility.* Providers are important members of the communities in which they operate. Their employees and their customers are part of the community. Providers continually strive to find ways to improve their social responsibility—through environmental initiatives, supplier diversity initiatives, and other social responsibility activities. While these items may not win you the sale by themselves, any advantages in these areas could be a key differentiator and one that wins you the deal if all other buying factors are close.

If these are the general goals of most sourcing initiatives, then it is up to you to determine how your solution uniquely helps the customer achieve these goals. I talk more about this in coming chapters. However, it's good to keep these broad sourcing objectives in mind as you think about selling and defending your value.

If you are used to engaging with users, whether physicians or others, it may be a little awkward dealing with economic buyers like materials management or the supply chain. A helpful technique is to ask good questions. These should align with how the professional buyer thinks about buying goods and services, and what "jobs" the professional buyer is trying to get done.

As an example, you could take each of the areas listed above and develop questions for your business. You can consider each of the areas as jobs the professional buyer is trying to get done. For instance, managing supply-chain risk is a job the buyer is trying to get done. Usually, this is a very important job for the buyer. Supply chain disruptions are a big headache for many buyers.

If your closest competitor has experienced production issues, supply problems, or delivery issues, you should be probing the buyer about how important supply continuity is to them. You could also ask the buyer what happens when there is a backorder or supply issue:

- What happens to the hospital operations?

- Do they need to find alternative supplies? What does this cost?

- Are procedures postponed? How does it impact scheduling?

- Does the hospital need to hold excess inventory?

This is not an exhaustive list, but you should get the point. Good questions can help you uncover potential sources of value and lead the buyer where you want to go.

HOW BUYERS DECIDE WHERE TO FOCUS

Strategic sourcing is not an event. Rather, it is a process for continually improving the value that comes from suppliers. In the best-run organizations, it is a fact-based and cross-functional process. It is usually put in place only where the materials management or supply chain organization has reached greater maturity.

One of the first steps in any strategic sourcing process is organizing all of the spend into like categories. This simply means organizing everything the provider buys into buckets, or groupings. For example, janitorial suppliers might be a category of spend. Likewise, bagels and breakfast foods might be a category of supply.

Beyond these mundane categories are categories for things like spinal implants, cardiac stents, and all the other items hospitals purchase. There's no exact science to the categorization of spend or the exact number of categories to have. As an example, one very large hospital system segmented its spend into 300 different categories.[7]

Once the hospital has categorized the supply items, it will then need to decide where to focus. In other words, across the 300 categories of spend, where should the hospital start? You may be asking yourself why a salesperson should care about this. If you understand how the supply chain thinks about this, you can better anticipate when your supply category will come up for bid and how best to prepare for this.

In general, providers use eight factors to decide where to focus for upcoming sourcing initiatives.[8] As a supplier, the net result would be an RFP, an e-auction, or some other request to bid on the business. The eight factors are as follows.

1. *Total spend.* This is the total amount of spend that the category represents. Obviously, the greater the spend, the more the hospital will be interested in going after this category.

2. *Last sourcing initiative.* Categories that have never been sourced or that haven't been sourced in a long time are more likely to see a sourcing initiative than those for which there has been a recent sourcing initiative.

3. *Available benchmarking.* If high-level benchmarking data show little opportunity, the supply-chain or materials-management team will not want to waste their time. However, if benchmarking shows significant opportunity, the category will be a big candidate.

4. *Rate of technology change.* Categories with rapid technology change should be sourced more frequently than ones with little change.

5. *Category complexity.* Categories for which it is easy for the customer to conduct a value analysis are more likely candidates than those for which conducting value analysis is difficult.

6. *Number of physicians.* Categories that have many physicians or departments that need to be aligned are more difficult than those with few physicians or just one department.

7. *Physician–user alignment.* Spend categories where the physician or user is aligned on lowering costs are much better candidates for sourcing initiates than others.

8. *Physician–supplier relationship.* Supply chain and materials management see opportunity in categories where there are or have historically been strong physician–supplier relationships. There is a general belief that the hospital has been overpaying for supplies where this dynamic is in place.

Figure 4.1. Sourcing focus diagnostic

1	Factor	5	Your Score
Little	**Total Spend**	Significant	
Very recent	**Last Sourcing**	Never	
Little	**Spend Benchmarks**	Opportunity	
Little	**Technology Change**	Often	
High	**Complexity/Switching Costs**	Low	
High	**Number of Users**	Smaller	
Doesn't care	**User Cost Mindset**	Lower costs	
Weak	**User–Supplier Relationship**	Strong	
		Total Score	

30–40 points: High likelihood of sourcing
16–29 points: Moderate likelihood of sourcing
0–15 points: Low likelihood of sourcing

These eight areas should give you some insights into potential sourcing initiatives. Pay close attention to any changes in these areas. For example, if you sell to a hospital that has just acquired its physician practices and you haven't seen a request for proposal (RFP) in many years, you should get prepared.

Figure 4.1 is a simple diagnostic to help you prepare. Each of the eight categories can be scored from 1 to 5. This isn't meant to be an exact science but rather to provide you with some guidance. Score each of the criteria and total your score. If you score between 30 and 40 points, there's a high likelihood you will see lots of sourcing initiative focused on you. If you score under 20, you shouldn't be worried.

CUSTOMERS' VIEW OF YOUR SALES BAG

Once the customer decides where to focus, they then need to decide on how to attack the supply category. Using the 300 categories of supply as an example, the materials management team will attack each of the categories in different ways. This is because the supply and buying dynamics are different for each category.

As an example, consider buying office supplies and orthopaedic implants. These are very different categories of spend. There may be very powerful physicians who have years of training invested in using a particular type of implant. Getting these physicians to agree on switching suppliers could be a challenge. Contrast this with buying office supplies. While some people may become upset at switching office-supply vendors, this switch would be much less difficult than switching implantable medical devices.

A simple category-segmentation model is presented in Figure 4.2. The vertical axis is the relative amount of money the customer spends on your good or service. This is not the price, but the amount of spending. The horizontal axis is the supply dynamics. This is composed of four factors:

- *Physician preference.* This is the strength of physician or clinician preference in the buying decision for the item. Basic commodities like gauze and packs and gowns may have very low physician preference.

On the other hand, new implant technologies may have very high physician preference. Also, physicians who have been trained to use a specific technology may strongly prefer one vendor over another.

- *Sources of supply.* This is the number of qualified suppliers who can provide that good or service. For some products or solutions there is only one real supplier. For other products or solutions there are dozens of potential suppliers who can provide a similar quality of product, service, and delivery.

- *Switching costs.* Switching costs are the costs the customer incurs when switching from one supplier or supply item to another. Switching costs can be things like training, inventory, and administrative costs. Switching costs can also include purchasing "leaks." Purchasing leaks occur when the buyer switches from one vendor to another but is unable to move the required portion of the business to the new supplier. For example, the materials management team may negotiate a new deal and agree to move 80% of a given supply item to a new supplier. In exchange for switching, the new supplier would provide a low price. However, if materials management is only able to switch 50% of the business to the new supplier, it would be buying the rest from other vendors, presumably at higher prices. Professional buyers refer to this as "leakage."

- *Critical to care.* This means how critical the item is to patient care or satisfaction. Supply items have very different impacts on this dimension. In the diagnostics industry, for example, a new diagnostic test that can accurately diagnose an ischemic stroke would have a very different impact on care than a routine cholesterol test.

Figure 4.2 provides a framework for thinking about your sales and negotiation strategy within the context of the provider's sourcing strategy. It's important to think about whatever you are selling from the perspective of how the account overall would view your supply item. You should not view this from the perspective of the professional buyer alone.

Many professional buyers will treat you or your supply item as if it is a commodity. They may actually tell you "these are all the same—they're a commodity." However, don't fall into that trap. This is a typical negotiation tactic. They want you to think price is the only thing that matters.

Figure 4.2. Supply category segmentation

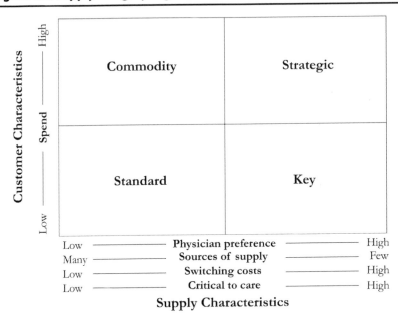

Supply Characteristics

Note. Adapted from D. Bueler, "Supplier Segmentation—The Tool for Differentiation and Results," 91st Annual International Supply Management Conference, May 2006.

You may fall into any of four broad categories. Each corresponds to a different area of focus from professional buyers. If you have many items in your sales bag, they probably fall into many different categories. It's not uncommon for products within the same broad product family (e.g., sutures, stents, immunoassays, orthopaedic implants) to fall into different quadrants on this chart. So be careful to map at a granular-enough level that makes sense for your business.

What follows is a general description of each of the quadrants with some insights for selling.

Commodity Items

Supply items that fall into the upper left corner are commodities. These are a relatively high-budget spend and are characterized by little clinician preference, many sources of supply, and lower switching costs. These are items that get sourced frequently. However, even when the core product or service falls into this category, these items can still be differentiated. When the core product becomes less differentiated, it is often the associated services and other areas where the real value difference is created. We will talk more about this in the chapter on offering strategy.

Strategic Items

Items in the upper right corner are strategic items. These are also high-budget spend items but are characterized by a high degree of physician or user preference. For these strategic items there are also fewer sources of supply and higher switching costs. Many items that were considered physician-preference items (PPIs) fall into this category. These are items that were traditionally hard for the supply chain to attack since it required alignment with the physicians. With all of the changes happening under healthcare reform, this category has been in focus as a sourcing opportunity for many buyers.

Key Items

The supply items that would fall into the lower right corner are relatively low-budget, but high-preference, items. For these items there may also be fewer sources of supply and higher switching costs. These key items are usually "under the radar" because they don't represent a lot of spending and because for these it is hard to switch suppliers. For some items, there may be only one real supplier. For suppliers, this is a great place to be.

Standard Items

Finally, in the lower left corner are low-budget and low-preference items. These are also items that are relatively easy to switch. From a buyer's perspective, these items don't represent big savings opportunities.

Link Supply Segmentation to Sales and Marketing Strategy

One way to think about the framework in Figure 4.2 is that this is the buyer's playbook. This is the lens through which the buyer views what you sell. If you were to follow a typical new-to-the-world product from introduction to maturity, it would follow a common path in Figure 4.2. The product would start in the lower right corner as a key item. As you became successful and grew your business, it would hopefully become a strategic item.

Over time, as competition enters the market, the item may evolve into a commodity. This is when the physical product is less differentiated and there are many competitive solutions. It is also at this stage that the buyer may have a lot of experience with the item and be more willing to take risks on lower priced suppliers. This is when price seems to become a much more important factor in the buying decision.

From a selling and marketing perspective, you should be adapting your strategy as your items evolve from one category to the next. For example, as an item moves into the commodity quadrant, value differences often shift from the product to the services and support provided. It's at this stage that you should be communicating the differentiation of your services and using services as trades in the negotiation. I talk more about this in the offering strategy chapter.

Anticipate Sourcing Strategies

The customer's sourcing strategy is likely to be different depending on the quadrant your goods or services fall into. Likewise, the buying center, or group of people involved in making the purchasing decision, is likely to be different. For example, for items that are considered commodities, procurement or materials management is more likely to play a more significant role in the decision process than for items that are considered strategic. This should influence your pricing, offering, and value communication strategy.

From an overall supply-chain and strategic-sourcing perspective, the provider will likely take a different approach to sourcing the items that fall into each quadrant. For items in the commodity quadrant, the provider will seek to consolidate spend, standardize, reduce inventory, and shrink handling costs. Since supply items in this quadrant are relatively high-budget spend items, they naturally should receive a high degree of attention. The provider may also look to group purchasing organization (GPO) contracts to standardize and reduce costs.

Figure 4.3. Strategic sourcing tactics

	Commodity	Strategic
	• Consolidate spend • Use purchasing alliances • Cost benchmarking • Supplier managed inventory	• Align incentives • Invest in relationship • Appropriate utilization • Long-term agreements • Involvement in innovation • Leverage competencies
	Standard	Key
	• Consolidate spend • Standardize purchasing • Use purchasing alliances • Minimize transaction costs	• Long-term agreements • Appropriate utilization • Optimize supply chain costs

Customer Characteristics — High / Spend / Low

Low	Physician preference	High
Many	Sources of supply	Few
Low	Switching costs	High
Low	Critical to care	High

Supply Characteristics

For strategic items, suppliers will take a different approach because the supply characteristics are different. In recent years, providers and payers have become more sophisticated in attacking the costs and uses of medical technologies. This is particularly true for high-spend, high-physician-preference items. These are items that would fall into the strategic category. In the US, for example, demonstration projects by CMS have shown that aligning incentives between physicians and hospitals reduces both prices and the use of expensive PPIs.[9]

There are a number of sourcing tools and approaches providers can use to reduce costs, ensure appropriate use, and manage suppliers. The sourcing tactics are summarized in Figure 4.3.

These are the tactics that you and your sales organization will encounter in the buying process:

- *Consolidate spend.* Reduce the number of suppliers and consolidate spend to negotiate better pricing and terms.

- *Use purchasing alliances.* Use group purchasing organization (GPO) contracts or regional purchasing alliances to gain more favorable pricing and terms. In the US, many hospitals and hospital systems are forming regional buying organizations to leverage their buying power.

- *Cost benchmarking.* Conduct frequent benchmarking of costs to identify savings opportunities.

- *Supplier-managed inventory.* Require suppliers to hold and manage inventory to reduce inventory carrying costs and costs associated with managing inventory.

- *Minimize transaction costs.* Use electronic ordering, inventory replenishment, and other tools to reduce transaction costs.

- *Appropriate utilization.* Align physicians and users on patient-selection criteria and usage guidelines to manage expensive technologies.

- *Align incentives.* Use various mechanisms to align the financial interests of physicians with the provider.

- *Long-term agreements.* Negotiate long-term agreements to gain price concessions and to ensure supply.

- *Involvement in innovation.* Gain access to suppliers' innovation pipeline, including access to clinical trials.

- *Invest in relationship.* Develop deep relationships with suppliers to leverage competencies and access resources.

- *Leverage competencies.* Seek access to suppliers' competencies that can help the provider compete more effectively.

- *Optimize supply chain costs.* Ensure supply chain is managed to take costs out and to optimize cost position.

- *Price cap.* Establish the maximum price the customer will pay for a solution. Any vendor who wants to sell to the customer must be at or below the cap. This is usually used for strategic or key supply items where the customer can't standardize on suppliers.

GETTING READY FOR STRATEGIC SOURCING TACTICS

One of the exercises you should perform as a business is to map where you think your customers would place your key offerings in Figure 4.2. It is possible that different segments of customers would view your products or services differently. For instance, in some segments your product or service may account for a relatively larger percentage of the customer's overall supplier spend.

This means you may feel more intense pricing pressure in that segment. So be sure to conduct the exercise at the segment level. After that, spend some time ensuring that your selling and pricing tactics are aligned with the tactics that procurement will likely use against you.

I have performed this exercise many times with sales teams. There are a couple of things to consider. First, your assessment of your sales bag should be fair and reasonable. You shouldn't map your products to where you hope they would be viewed.

Likewise, consider how the account as a whole would view your supply item. Of course, smart purchasing people are trained to persuade you that your product or solution is a commodity. This is one of the standard negotiation tactics. Take a balanced view that includes how the account *overall* would view your supply items.

In later chapters I talk about procurement tactics and tricks. Procurement people are typically skilled negotiators. They'll use a variety of tools and tactics to try to keep you off balance. These are meant to change the balance of power in the negotiations and to extract more value (e.g., price) from you. After all, driving a price concession is a simple and easy way for the procurement person to record savings.

Understanding how procurement views your supply items is critical for preparing for negotiations and the selling opportunity. If you enter negotiations without understanding this, you end up being merely reactive.

For example, if you are the incumbent supplier providing a supply item that would be considered strategic in Figure 4.3, you have to carefully consider switching costs. Very high switching costs create a barrier to change. You can use this in negotiations. Alternatively, if you sell a strategic item and are dealing with a prospective customer, realize that switching costs can be a barrier. If the customer is relatively happy with the incumbent, it's much easier for the buyer to reduce the incumbent's price than it is for the customer to switch suppliers.

KEY TAKEAWAYS

- Hospital and healthcare supply chains tend to lag far behind other industries in their capabilities.

- One of the tools more sophisticated supply chains use is strategic sourcing. This is simply a strategic approach to managing suppliers and the buying process. You should understand your customers' strategic sourcing goals and use this in the selling process.

- The better you prepare, the better your chances of selling your value and defending your value against strategic sourcing tactics.

- Being prepared means understanding how buyers think about what you sell. It also means trying to anticipate the sourcing tactics they are likely to use against you. With these insights, you can better prepare to win.

NOTES

1. www.brainyquote.com (accessed November 2, 2013).

2. K. Montgomery and E. Schneller, "Hospital Strategies for Orchestrating Selection of Physician Preference Items," *Milbank Quarterly* 85.2 (2007).

3. Ibid.

4. C. Dominick and S. Lunney, *The Procurement Game Plan* (J. Ross Publishing, 2012).

5. B. Herman, "4 Pressing Financial Issues Facing Hospital Executives Today," *Becker's Hospital Review* [Blog], www.beckershospitalreview.com, April 19, 2012 (Accessed November 1, 2013).

6. See AHRMM.org.

7. D. Hargraves, "Making a Good Supplier Better Through Sustainable Supplier Development," presentation at Next Level Purchasing Conference, September 2013.

8. Adapted from E. Pursell, "Sourcing Physician Preference Supplies," Physician Preference Item Management Conference, March 18, 2008, asu.edu (accessed November 2, 2013).

9. B. Herman, "2 Major Lessons From CMS' Bundled Payment ACE Demonstration," *Becker's Hospital Review* [Blog], www.beckershospitalreview.com, April 3, 2012 (accessed November 1, 2013).

Chapter | 5

NAVIGATE BUYING COMMITTEES

It's not what you look at that matters, it's what you see.

—Henry David Thoreau[1]

Picture an automobile assembly line. Rather than the orderly process many of us have seen in the news or in movies, imagine a chaotic car assembly. Visualize a process where the workers do whatever they want. For example, imagine there's no common way to attach the doors to the car. Each worker who is assigned to attach doors does it differently.

Also, imagine this same process with the workers using different suppliers for all of the parts that go into making the car. The workers get to decide what supplier they want to use. There would be multiple suppliers for the doors, for example. While each door supplier may have similar specifications, each supplier's product might be a bit different. The auto manufacturer would have to hold lots of inventory because of all the different suppliers.

What kind of car would this process produce? There probably would be much variation. Sometimes the car might be very good; other times it might be terrible. You can imagine that there would be lots of rework or repair after the car left the factory.

Also, how easy would it be to control quality and costs in this example? It would be a nightmare. There would be no standard process for assembling the cars. Using many different suppliers would create a lot of waste. It would be hard to identify which supplier was best for each part. The fact that each worker bought from whatever supplier he or she wanted means there would be little leverage of the manufacturer's purchasing power.

Clearly, no modern manufacturer would run its business this way. It would go out of business quickly because of the waste, poor quality, and rework. However, this is how many hospitals have run for the past century. Experts point out that there are few standard care processes in many hospitals.[2] Also, for many supply items, individual physicians have decided what supply to use, and there has been little standardization.

Obviously, comparing healthcare to automobile assembly is a crude analogy. It is not intended to de-value the work of talented physicians and other caregivers. However, the point is that hospitals have to bring some order and standardization to care in order to improve outcomes and reduce costs. In fact, many hospitals have recognized this challenge and are turning to lean manufacturing concepts to improve quality of care and outcomes. One basic lean principle is to create standard work, which simply means agreeing on the standard processes for patient care.

Standard work would include standardization on the technologies used to care for patients. This doesn't mean choosing only one supplier for hip implants, for instance. However, standard work would mean standard guidelines for which implant to use for various types of patients.

Value analysis or buying committees are a sign that a hospital is serious about improving outcomes, enhancing quality, and reducing costs. Value analysis or buying committees often allow the hospital to find the best technologies to meet their cost, quality, and outcome goals. This is not to take the decisions out of the hands of individual physicians, but rather to have evidence-based, expert consensus on the right clinical pathways and technologies to treat patients. This gives the hospital some opportunity to standardize on process and suppliers.

As the buying process increasingly involves committee-based buying decisions, it's important to understand these groups. The purpose of this chapter is to provide insights into these committees, their decision process, and how you can navigate them.

BUYING COMMITTEE BASICS

Buying committees usually consist of a cross-functional team of clinicians, finance, materials management, and other hospital personnel. These committees go by many different names:

- *Pharmacy and therapeutics (P&T) committee:* focused on pharmacy formulary and purchasing decisions.

- *Capital budget committee:* usually focused on evaluating capital purchase requests.

- *Medical equipment committee:* focused on evaluating medical equipment purchasing.

- *Value analysis committee (VAC) or value analysis team (VAT):* generally focused on medical and surgical supply evaluations.

- *Department or service-line-level buying committee:* can be buying committees for specific areas (e.g., laboratory).

- *Strategic sourcing team:* ad hoc team that focuses on buying a specific item or category of supplies (e.g., food services).

Committee-based buying is not new to hospitals. In the hospital pharmacy, there have been P&T committees for some time. In fact, P&T committees were introduced almost a century ago to discuss in-hospital drug use.[3]

One of the key roles of the P&T committee is management of the formulary and authorization and restriction of new drugs. The P&T committee normally focuses on safety, clinical appropriateness, and cost containment in making formulary decisions. Managing costs and the pharmacy budget are often key buying decisions.[4]

Whereas committee buying is not new for most hospitals, the evolution of committee buying in some areas outside of the pharmacy is relatively new. In the medical and surgical supply areas of the hospital, buying committees are now being used more widely. In this area, the buying committee is often called a value analysis committee.

According to the Association for Healthcare Value Analysis Professionals, value analysis is a multi-disciplinary approach to ensuring optimal patient outcomes through clinical efficacy of healthcare products and services for the greatest financial value.[5] In other words, value analysis and value committees try to balance costs, quality, and outcomes.

The degree of influence and scope of the VAC varies across hospitals. According to studies, approximately two-thirds of hospitals in the US use some kind of VAC to assist in purchasing decision-making.[6] VACs function similarly to P&T committees.

How purchasing committees are used varies widely across hospitals. Even in the pharmacy, where hospitals have a long history of using P&T committees, there is wide variation. Studies show that there is a general lack of standardized procedures or methods for decision making.[7] This means that you need to do your homework and understand how the committee at your customer operates.

DETERMINE THE PURPOSE AND STRUCTURE

Purpose and Composition of Value or Buying Committee

Buying committees serve many different functions. In some hospitals, the committee is the decider for major purchases. In this case, you might want to map the committee itself to try to understand the relative influence of each of its members.

For example, a VAC may include members from many parts of the hospital:

- Administration/Finance
- Materials & Supply Chain Management (MSCM)
- Purchasing
- Nursing
- Medical Staff
- Infection Control
- Clinical Engineering
- Staff Training & Development
- Information Technology

- Facilities Management
- Quality

On some committees, perhaps just one or two people are the true deciders. The other members may be able to reject a particular supply or supplier but not accept any. For example, if you were selling a new piece of capital equipment that connected to a hospital's information system, the Information Technology department might be able to say no to your product because of technical requirements for interfacing with the hospital computer system. However, the IT department may have little influence if multiple vendors can successfully connect to the hospital information system.

Other committees may follow formal rules regarding how voting happens and who gets to vote. The committees may also adhere to formal rules with respect to membership. The size, complexity, history, and culture of the organization will often dictate how formally or informally the committee operates. You can find much of the committee information for your hospital via the Internet or by asking the right questions.

It's also important to determine the committee's purpose. Sometimes the VAC is involved in buying decisions for a particular supply category or item.

In many cases, however, the committee really acts like a continuous improvement team. Its role is to continually drive costs out and improve the value gained from the supply base. In these cases, the committee not only makes decisions about specific categories of spend but also searches for cost savings opportunities.

As an example, one hospital system defined the mission of its buying related committees thus: "to bring a diverse perspective from our various Hospital and Clinical departments and challenge current practices, [to] promote innovative solutions and to advance the hospital to the next generation of Supply Chain optimization and savings."[8]

Structure and Governance of Committee

One thing you should do, if you haven't already, is identify the committees at the hospital you call on. As mentioned, at some hospitals or hospital systems a multitude of committees are involved in purchasing decisions. You should try to clearly understand their scope, their charter, and their goals. Figure 5.1 is a simplified example from one hospital.[9]

Figure 5.1. Hospital buying committees example

Product Review	Impact on Hospital	Who Decides . . .
• Clinical assessment • Financial review • Quality impact • Healthcare reform impact • Safety review • Strategic impact evaluation • Supporting evidence	**Low** (less than $100K in new costs) **Moderate** (less than $500K in new costs) **High** ($500K or greater in new costs)	**Value Analysis Committee** **Service Line Committee** **Executive Committee**

In this case, the health system has a VAC that handles purchasing decisions that have a new cost impact of less than $100,000 annually. Decisions that cost between $100,000 and $500,000 go to the service-line committee. Supply or purchasing decisions that incur more than $500,000 in new costs go to an executive committee. Each hospital, integrated delivery network (IDN), or system will have different rules depending on its size, culture, purchasing maturity, and organizational structure.

From a sales perspective, you should find a coach in the organization to help guide you. Much of this information may be available on the hospital's website. Some basics questions to ask are as follows:

- Do you have a VAC?

- What is the committee's mission?

- What type of purchasing decisions does the committee get involved in?

- Are there formal rules or cut-offs for the decisions they are involved in?

- Are there any other committees that are involved in purchasing decisions besides the VAC?

- If so, what are the other committees, and how do they operate?

- How does the committee make decisions?

Identify Committee Members and Process

Once you identify the committees and their basic governance, you should identify the individuals on the committee. Pay close attention, in particular, to whether there are physicians on the committee. The committee's composition can sometimes signal how decisions are made.

In some situations, the physician on the committee may be a highly respected thought leader or department head. In other cases, he or she could simply be a physician who is less busy than the other physicians. In some cases, the physician may have little experience with the particular item being sourced. For example, at a cardiovascular service-line level, a surgeon may lead the committee but have no direct experience with products in a specific area like interventional cardiology.

You should also try to understand the committee process. Is it a closed committee? In other words, does the committee restrict vendor access? Or is it a committee process that expects vendors to come and present clinical, outcomes, and cost data? Knowing this well in advance is critical. You should also try to understand the committee calendar and review process. Good questions to ask are ones like these:

- How frequently does the committee meet?

- Does the committee hold regularly scheduled meetings, or is it ad hoc?

- Does every committee member usually attend?

- Who chairs the committee?

- Who are all the people on the committee?

- Do they follow formal policies and templates?

- How are decisions made? Is there a vote?

Getting this right—identifying who is on the committee—could mean the difference between winning and losing. For example, assume you had a new technology that was going to greatly impact some of the value-based purchasing incentives that the hospital receives from Medicare. If the committee was composed of a physician, a purchasing agent, and an administrator from the service line, you could be in trouble. It is possible that none of those players understands how the new CMS value-based purchasing works in enough detail to appreciate the positive impact of your technology. If you can't find a way to influence them or to bring the right information to their attention, you will have lost the opportunity.

While every hospital is a little different, almost all buying committees—VACs, capital committees, new technology committees, and P&T committees—now include a financial representative. Usually this person is a chief financial officer or finance director. For smaller accounts, this person can also be the chief operating officer.

With thin margins and all of the financial pressure on hospitals, administrators have realized that they need to tightly control costs. The financial evaluation of supply items is now a primary factor in buying decisions. As one cardiovascular service-line leader said, "Finance leaders are playing a much bigger role than they did even a few years ago. Finance conducts the financial analysis and says, 'We're not buying it unless you convince me otherwise.'"[10]

One of the reasons for identifying VAC or buying committee members and the committee process is to work in advance of any formal meeting, much like a lobbyist works in Washington. In Washington, lobbyists are busy working all the key decision makers in advance of key Congressional meetings to educate and advocate for their position. Then Senator John F. Kennedy described lobbyists as "in many cases expert technicians capable of examining complex and difficult subjects in a clear, understandable fashion."[11]

The point is that if you wait until the committee meeting to try to influence the decision, you've missed a big opportunity. You need to think like a Washington lobbyist and clearly understand the key stakeholders and decision process. With this in mind, you can implement a plan to educate and influence key committee members well in advance of any meeting.

LEARN HOW THE COMMITTEE MAKES DECISIONS

You need to understand how the committee makes decisions. Do they follow a formal process, or an informal process? The key points to understand are these:

- How do they decide to look at a particular supply area? Is the decision initiated by a vendor? Is it part of their normal strategic sourcing process?

- When evaluating a supply category, how do they choose a specific vendor?

- What specific metrics do they look at?

- Is it a process where they vote? Does each member have a vote? Is it a consensus-type process?

- Or is it a process that is highly influenced or controlled by one individual?

Information to Influence the Committee

After you better understand how the decision is made, you should determine what questions the committee asks and the information or metrics they use to make decisions. A metric could be financial, clinical, or process related. For example, they might look at the total cost per discharge. On the other hand, it could be a clinical or operational metric, like length of stay. You should learn about the inputs they consider when making buying decisions. Armed with this information, you will be well prepared to communicate the value your solution provides.

Questions Committees Ask

The questions the committee asks will vary based on what they are buying, their goals, and the buying behavior of the account. In general, some common types of questions will be asked. These are listed by committee type below.[12]

Realize that the committee at your accounts may be called something different. These questions are generic. Obviously, the committee you are dealing with may ask very specific questions related to the solution you are providing. For example, a committee buying laboratory equipment might ask about the ability of the equipment to handle stat as opposed to routine testing demands.

P&T Committee (Pharmacy)

- Is there a compelling need to add the drug to our formulary?

- What is the evidence to support the claims for this drug?

- What safety issues need to be considered?

- If placed on the formulary, what is the potential for misuse or overuse?

- Can we justify the cost of this drug? What is the cost per discharge?

- What is the impact on value-based purchasing and quality metrics?

- What are the strength and quality of evidence and information available to the committee?

- What are the status and quality of the review process and use at our institution?

VAC (Medical/Surgical Supplies)

- Do we need this item for patient care?

- Are there meaningful clinical differences?

- Is there an opportunity to reduce supplier costs?

- Can we improve outcomes or quality with this supplier?

- What process or workflow improvements might this supply item provide?

- Is there an impact on inventory or handling?

- Are there other cost-reduction opportunities?

- Does the supply item create new service-line or revenue-capture opportunities?

- Are there strategic benefits to acquiring the supply item?

- Can the cost of the supply item be justified?

- What is the impact on value-based purchasing and quality metrics?

- What evidence exists to support the clinical and financial claims?

- Is there an opportunity for misuse?

- Are there patient safety issues to consider?

New Medical Equipment Buying Committee

- Is there an existing device that is at the "end of life" and that needs to be replaced or upgraded to improve the quality of patient care delivery?

- Will the device meet the clinical/patient care need?

- Is the device compatible with the existing inventory (for example, user training/experience, spare parts inventory, service contracts)?
- Is the device compatible with the existing infrastructure (software, hardware)?
- Is the device capable of wireless communication and electronic medical records integration?
- Are there strategic benefits of the device/technology?
- Can the cost of the device/technology be justified?
- What are the operational, workflow, or cost savings?
- What is the impact on value-based purchasing and quality metrics?
- What is the overall return on investment?

Capital Committee

- Will the capital item meet or improve clinical/patient care needs?
- Will the capital item improve patient satisfaction or the hospital brand?
- Is it a strategic investment?
- What is the impact on value-based purchasing and quality metrics?
- Does the capital investment reduce costs or improve workflow or productivity?
- What is the overall return on investment?

You can use this list as a starting point. However, it is always good to ask the customer what types of questions the committee asks. These insights should help you to prepare the right answers to the questions to best leverage your value.

Potential Value Metrics Used by Committee

The value metrics used to make decisions will vary depending on what is being purchased, how the institution is reimbursed, and the practices of the provider. In later chapters I describe in detail how to quantify your value. In general, you need to think about the differentiated value of your solution in five ways:

- *Cost.* Does your solution or technology cost more, or less, from a total cost of ownership (TCO) perspective? TCO is simply the cost to purchase, use, maintain, and dispose of the solution.

- *Quality/Outcomes.* Does your product or solution have a positive impact on patient outcomes or quality?

- *Time.* This is the impact of your solution on the time involved in diagnosing or treating patients. Is speed to diagnosis important? Is the procedure cycle time important?

- *Revenue.* Does your product or solution have some kind of impact on the institution's revenue? This gets tricky and will depend, in part, on how the institution is reimbursed and the payer mix. Impacts on revenue, like the incentives under value-based purchasing, should be fairly straightforward.

- *Social responsibility.* Hospitals are keenly aware of the impact of their business on the local community. Most hospitals focus on helping the local community through supplier diversity and environmental initiatives. These could be leverage points for you as a supplier.

Obviously, your solution may have benefits that impact multiple categories of value. For example, your solution may reduce readmissions to the hospital (improve outcomes), a reduction for which the hospital gets an extra incentive from the payer (revenue). In general, there are a number of generic metrics that the hospital could use to evaluate your solution. You need to ask how they assess value and what measures or metrics they use.

You should also not just rely on the feedback from the hospital about the specific metrics they use. There may be other important value-related metrics that they should be looking at. For example, some authors argue that many P&T committees have a very narrow focus and need to reinvent themselves for the new world of value-based purchasing.[13]

Rather than relying purely on the customer to tell you the value metrics, you might find it helpful to think broadly about the types of metrics they should use. In other words, look at the potential metrics shown in Table 5.1 to determine whether you have an advantage in any of these areas. It's your chance to educate them about the value your solution brings.

Table 5.1 includes references to specific reimbursement incentives that have been included in the Affordable Care Act (ACA) in the US. These are meant as examples. Since reimbursement policy and payment are ever-changing, you should refer to CMS.gov for the most current reimbursement rules and policies impacting providers in the US.

If you are selling outside of the US, many of these metrics may be relevant, but you need to adapt them for your specific reimbursement model.

Table 5.1. Potential Value Metrics

Value category and metric	Description
Cost	
Budget impact or TCO (total cost of ownership)	Impact of the technology or solution on the hospital after accounting for cost offsets—increases or reductions in cost related to the use, maintenance, and disposal of the solution.
Supply costs as a percentage of reimbursement	Total supply costs for a procedure divided by total reimbursement. Shows what percentage of the payment is available to pay for overhead and labor.
Total inpatient case costs	Total cost of the case for inpatient care.
Cost per beneficiary or per capita	Cost to care for a patient over a defined period. May include inpatient, outpatient, and other costs. For example, under the accountable care program in the US, CMS will look at the cost per beneficiary over a 3-year period. It will include both inpatient and outpatient costs.

Value category and metric	Description
Quality/Outcomes	
Mortality/Morbidity	Impact of your technology or solution on patient mortality and morbidity. Obviously, having an advantage in one of these areas is great. It is even better if you can connect these differences to how the customer is reimbursed. The Affordable Care Act (ACA) in the US includes incentives tied to improving mortality.
Patient satisfaction / quality of life (QoL)	Impact of your solution on patient satisfaction or QoL. The ACA in the US includes providers' incentives tied to improving patient satisfaction. In addition, patient QoL is often used as a metric to evaluate different treatments or technologies.
Rate of 30-day readmissions	Percentage or absolute number of patients who are readmitted within 30 days. Under the initial value-based purchasing program from CMS (Centers for Medicare and Medicaid Services) in the US, the focus was on readmissions related to certain diagnoses.
Value-based purchasing	Impact on CMS value-based purchasing metrics such as patient satisfaction, clinical process measures, specific outcome metrics, and cost efficiency.
Time	
Turnaround time for diagnostic results	Time it takes to turn around a test result and provide an accurate diagnosis. This could be for in-vitro or in-vivo diagnostics.
Length of stay (LOS)	Time the patient stays in the hospital. Could be measured in total days or be broken out into components, such as ICU days and step-down units.
Procedure cycle time	Time it takes to complete a procedure. May be important when the service line has capacity constraints. For example, a busy hospital with a full operating-room schedule may value solutions that help it reduce procedure time.
Revenue	
Reduce penalty or reimbursement bonus	In the US, there are numerous potential penalties under value-based purchasing whereby the provider is penalized for poor quality. If you believe your solution will positively impact this, be prepared to have this conversation.

Value category and metric	Description
Service-line revenue growth	This is a tricky metric. Depending on how the customer is reimbursed and who the payer is, could be viewed as either positive or negative.
Social responsibility	
Supplier diversity	Many hospital supply chains have a focus on supplier diversity. This is simply promoting the development and growth of diverse suppliers. If you are a diverse supplier or your company has a strong program, this may be very important to the hospital.
Environmental impact	Hospital waste and environmental impact are big issues. Hospitals have a big impact on the environment. If you have an advantage in this area, be prepared to highlight this.

Role of Evidence

If you have an advantage in any of these metrics, that's great. The buying committee is likely to ask you for evidence to support your value claims. The degree of evidence the committee seeks will depend on the following:

- *Costs.* The amount of incremental costs or total spending related to the purchase. The greater the spending or new costs, the more important evidence will become.

- *Clinical risk.* The clinical risk involved in the decision. More risk will generally increase the level of evidence required.

- *Business risk.* The business or financial risk related to the decision. Increasing business risk will result in a desire for more evidence.

- *Complexity and change.* The amount of change required to benefit from your solution. Savvy customers know that any proposed savings or benefits from vendors exist only on paper until the solution is implemented. The more change required or the more complex the solution appears, the more the customer will be looking for evidence that other customers have achieved the benefits promised.

- *Their practices.* The policies or norms related to evidence for the purchase. Some customers are much more formal or academic in the use and evaluation of evidence. Other customers are more informal.

Each customer approaches evidence differently. As you engage with different members of the buying committee, it will be important to learn from them what types of evidence they expect.

Type and level of evidence will vary. Here are some general types and levels of evidence to consider:[14]

Figure 5.2. Types of evidence

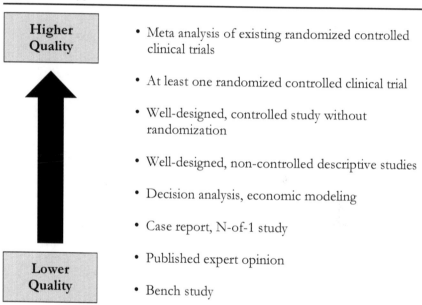

Higher Quality

- Meta analysis of existing randomized controlled clinical trials

- At least one randomized controlled clinical trial

- Well-designed, controlled study without randomization

- Well-designed, non-controlled descriptive studies

- Decision analysis, economic modeling

- Case report, N-of-1 study

- Published expert opinion

Lower Quality

- Bench study

KEY TAKEAWAYS

- Hospitals face tremendous pressure to reduce costs and improve quality. A buying committee is a cross-functional group that brings a diverse perspective to supplier-selection, cost-reduction, and quality-improvement decisions.

- Buying committees go by many different names. These include P&T committee, VAC, and capital committee.

- There is much variation across hospitals in terms of the structure and use of buying committees.

- Most hospitals have some form of VAC in place. The use of VACs will likely grow over time as the market evolves.

- It's important for suppliers to know and understand the VAC's structure, composition, purpose, and decision process.

- Smart suppliers should be prepared with a full breadth of metrics to help educate the customer on how their solution will impact the customer's business and key metrics.

- Having a coverage plan and strategy to connect with various members of the buying committee will be important in many selling scenarios.

NOTES

1. www.brainyquote.com (accessed February 7, 2014).

2. C. Berczuk, "The Lean Hospital," *The Hospitalist*, June 2008 (accessed November 2, 2013).

3. D. Shulkin, "Reinventing the Pharmacy and Therapeutics Committee," *Pharmacy and Therapeutics* 37.11 (November 2012): 623–24, 649 (accessed November 2, 2013).

4. Ibid.

5. See AHVAP.org.

6. G. Aston and S. Hoppszallern, "Preference Matters," *Hospital and Health Networks*, October 2009.

7. G. D. Schiff, W. L. Galanter, J. Duhig, M. J. Koronkowski, A. E. Lodolce, et al. "A Prescription for Improving Drug Formulary Decision Making," *PLoS Med* 9.5 (2012). doi:10.1371/journal.pmed.1001220.

8. See University of Connecticut Health Center Value Analysis Program, http://opa.uchc.edu/valueA/product_apr_policy.htm (accessed November 2, 2013).

9. Adapted from "The Benefits of a Successful Value Analysis Program" [Webcast], WellStar, www.iienet.org (accessed November 2, 2013).

10. C. Provines, "Smart Purchasing: Evolving Hospital Buying and Implications for Suppliers" (Working paper, 2014).

11. www.quotationsbook.com. (accessed February 8, 2014).

12. Adapted from Schiff et al., "A Prescription for Improving Drug Formulary Decision Making "; and D. Bradley, "Special Report: Purchasing Committees Place Medical Devices on Trial," *DotMed Daily News*, 2012, http://www.dotmed.com/ (accessed November 2, 2013).

13. Shulkin, "Reinventing the Pharmacy and Therapeutics Committee."

14. Adapted from James M. Anderson Center for Health Systems Excellence, "Evidence Based Tools and Decision Making," Cincinnati Children's, www.Cincinnatichildrens.org (accessed November 2, 2013).

PART III

PREPARE TO SELL AND DEFEND VALUE

Chapter | 6

QUANTIFY YOUR VALUE

Price is what you pay. Value is what you get.

—Warren Buffet[1]

If you've been reading along, hopefully you will agree that things are changing dramatically in healthcare. The days of getting a physician interested in a new supply item, which offers a marginal improvement in some features, and then getting the supply on contract at a higher price are largely over. Buyers are becoming much more demanding.

This situation brings to mind the saying from those old Western movies, "there's a new sheriff in town." In this case, there's a new buyer in town—a buyer who wants to know what value you are providing. Don't assume that the buyer knows. It's up to you to help educate the buyer about the value that you bring.

Bringing value to your customer is also about being seen as an expert who can help the customer improve their business. The goal shouldn't be to highlight your value just to make a sale. Rather, the goal should be to offer new insights and solutions to help the customer make smarter decisions. This should lead to better business and clinical outcomes.

So, the value you bring is not just your product or solution. It's your sales team and the expertise they offer to help customers achieve better outcomes. If you work in sales, it's you and the expertise you bring.

What is value? Early in my career, I worked on a key account management team that managed contracting and pricing for a medical devices company in the United States. In the throes of customer negotiations, I would often hear key account executives say that we needed to give the customer "more value." I soon learned that this was a euphemism for "we need to lower our prices."

Price was often confused with value. Few in that business, including me at that time, understood the value we provided to customers. We had no real idea of the value we delivered, let alone having it quantified.

In other businesses I've worked in, senior executives would often use the word "value." Many confused product features with the value those features provide to customers. They mistakenly assumed that feature-rich products or an abundance of features describing our services created value for customers. Features are what the product is—facts and data about the product or solution.

Such companies are not unusual. Many suppliers struggle with quantifying their value. If you think this is an exaggeration, try this simple test. Take out a piece of paper. List all the key products or solutions you sell. Check off how many have a clear and quantified value proposition.

In simple terms, clear and quantified value means that you could sit with the customer and explain the financial impact of your solution on their business. If you're like most suppliers, you probably have many solutions in your sales bag that have no clear, quantified value proposition. This chapter will help you quantify your value.

TRANSLATE FEATURES AND BENEFITS INTO VALUE

In a workshop with healthcare suppliers, one supplier said, "We have great quality. This should be a key differentiator, but customers don't seem to care." When probed about how this "great quality" is communicated to customers, he described ISO certification, compliance with good manufacturing practices (GMPs), environmental practices, and other "features." How many modern suppliers don't offer these same features?

Every supplier who visits a provider says the same thing—"We have great quality." No one is going to say to the customer, "Our quality stinks."

"Great quality" is a broad statement. It needs to be real, differentiated, and believable for the customer. Ideally, it needs to be quantifiable.

Simple Example of Quantifying The "Value" of Quality

Let's use a simplified example of a hospital that is considering standardizing on point-of-care testing devices. These devices use a small hand-held or portable instrument and reagents to perform near-patient testing on blood or urine samples. The hospital may have 2,000 users of these devices scattered throughout the facility. The users are primarily the nurses who run the tests.

What does better quality mean for these devices? Rather than talk about ISO or GMPs, you need to make quality real. For this simple example, let's say there are two suppliers. One supplier has had past quality issues with its reagents. The other supplier has a nearly perfect manufacturing record with no recalls or back orders.

The supplier with no back orders or recalls could say that it has great quality. Based on the supplier's track record, the customer could find this claim believable. However, it is still not quantified. What does this claim actually mean for the customer's business?

Remember, one of the goals in quantifying your value is to educate the customer and help them make better purchasing and business decisions. One simple way the high-quality supplier could frame the value is to show what happens to the customer's business if there is a supply or quality problem. In this case, there would be a number of key impacts. The numbers in Figure 6.1 are illustrative to make the point.

Although this is a simplified example, hopefully it makes the point. Rather than say "we have better quality," the high-quality manufacturer could quantify the impact of poor quality. For simplicity's sake, we calculated only two of the possible costs of poor quality. In this case, the customer could incur at least $145,000 in costs if it chose a supplier who has the potential for supply issues. If you wanted to take this to the next step, you could calculate the probability of the supply problem happening.

Figure 6.1. Example: Financial impact of poor quality

What if there is a quality problem?	• Customer has to acquire backup devices and retrain the nursing staff
How many devices, and at what cost?	• Customer would need 50 new devices at $2,000 each; equals $100,000
How many nurses need to be trained?	• 2,000 nurses would have to spend 30 minutes each in training; equals 1,000 hours in total
What is nurses' rate & labor cost?	• Nurses are paid $45 per hour times 1,000 hours; retraining equals $45,000
What is total cost of quality issue?	• The total cost could be $100,000 for backup devices and $45,000 for training; equals $145,000

Connect Features and Benefits to Value

Customers are busy. They usually don't have the time or information needed to do their own value analysis. The exception might be for really large purchases or significant changes in clinical practice. Studies show that even the best purchasing organizations can only do a value analysis a third of the time.[2]

If you expect your customer to calculate your value for you, you will be in trouble. Furthermore, sometimes it's in the customer's best interest not to calculate your value for you. This way they don't have to recognize and pay for the value when negotiating with you.

So, you will have to connect the dots for the customer. You must translate features and benefits into value. Features are facts and data about a product or solution. These could be related to speed, uptime, ease of use, or certain clinical parameters. Features describe the product or solution—at a very basic level, and often in language or terms that the customer does not care about.

Benefits connect a feature to a customer need. Assume that a customer needs to improve operating room (OR) procedure cycle time because the hospital lacks sufficient OR capacity. If you have a solution, one of whose key features is its ease of use, you can translate this feature into a benefit. The benefit would be that it reduces the OR procedure cycle time through its better ease of use. Benefits are a step above features, but they still leave the customer to quantify value for themselves.

Quantifying value means taking features and benefits and translating them into monetary terms. In the above example, translating ease of use to lower OR procedure cycle time is great. The next step is to assign a monetary amount to that benefit. For example, if the reduction in OR procedure cycle time would allow the hospital to avoid building a new OR to handle an increased caseload, then the value could be framed as the capital expense avoided.

Figure 6.2. Translate features and benefits to value

	Features	Benefits	Value
What is it?	• Data and facts about the solution • Usually expressed in the supplier's language	• Describe how features help address customer needs • Expressed in language that is important to the customer	• Quantify the financial impact to the customer's business • Expressed in monetary terms (e.g., dollars)
Example	• The new operating room instrument has higher radial strength and greater flexibility	• Allows surgeons to reduce procedure cycle time by one half hour	• The reduced cycle time results in better scheduling and lower overtime for nurses = $100,000 annually

Figure 6.2 shows the translation from feature to benefit to value. For each of the key items in your sales bag, you should be able to make this clear for your customer.

TYPES OF VALUE IN HEALTHCARE

Before we jump into the process of quantifying value, it will help to think about value in the broadest context. Value can be defined in many ways. Value is usually quantifiable and is based on consequences or outcomes. It includes the economic, clinical, and other benefits provided to stakeholders. Last, value is always relative to some alternative. Figure 6.3 provides an integrated way to think about value in the healthcare market. There are three key elements of value.

Figure 6.3. Healthcare value pyramid

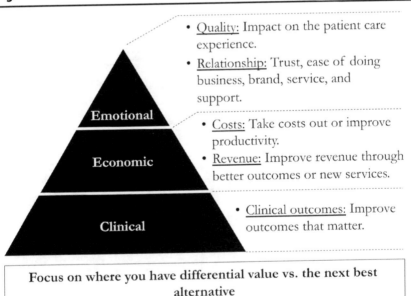

Emotional
- Quality: Impact on the patient care experience.
- Relationship: Trust, ease of doing business, brand, service, and support.

Economic
- Costs: Take costs out or improve productivity.
- Revenue: Improve revenue through better outcomes or new services.

Clinical
- Clinical outcomes: Improve outcomes that matter.

Focus on where you have differential value vs. the next best alternative

The first two elements, clinical and economic value, tend to be more rational and quantifiable. These elements are also ones that payers, policy makers, and other economic buyers look at when making decisions. The third element of value is meant to capture all of the intangible elements of value involved in purchase decisions. Despite the need for quantitative value, individuals and groups making buying decisions are human beings. This means that decisions often involve subjective and emotional factors as well.

The healthcare value pyramid is structured with clinical value as its foundation. Above clinical value is economic value. Finally, psychological or emotional value is at the top of the pyramid. Customers often prioritize the elements of value from bottom to top of the pyramid.

When there is a high unmet clinical need and one technology performs much better than the next best alternative, then clinical value becomes the leading form of value differentiation. When two technologies deliver similar clinical outcomes, then economic and emotional value become the basis for competition and value differentiation.

Clinical Value

The foundation of value in the healthcare markets is clinical value. Meaningful differences in clinical outcomes matter. This assumes, of course, that there is evidence to prove the clinical differences. These clinical improvements are attributes such as better safety, effectiveness, improved diagnosis, meeting a previously unmet need, and quality-of-life improvements. Since the primary purpose of a healthcare supply item is to improve human healthcare, this is the foundation of value for medical technologies.

Clinical value can be both anecdotal and evidence based. Anecdotal simply means that the caregivers can see the effects of the treatment or believe that the treatment or technology is delivering the intended benefits. Despite the movement to evidence-based medicine, much of clinical practice is still based on the perceptions and case history of individual clinicians. If the clinicians are able to directly observe the technology having an impact on patient outcomes, this is a powerful value element.

On the other hand, given the cost pressures in most countries around paying for healthcare, there is a significant movement towards evidence-based medicine. This is particularly true in markets where the government is the primary payer. The result is a need for suppliers to prove clinical value through evidence. So, while a healthcare supplier may believe that its technology has significant clinical value, without evidence it will be difficult to substantiate value.

Economic Value

Economic value represents the quantifiable savings or benefits in monetary terms of one technology or service compared with an alternative. Economic value can be described and calculated in a variety of ways, and through the use of many metrics and quantification techniques. These include total cost of ownership (TCO), budget impact modeling, and health economic metrics such as cost-effectiveness and cost-utility analysis. For the purposes of this book, we will focus on value from the provider perspective.

Psychological or Emotional Value

Psychological value includes things like brand, reputation, ease of doing business, ease of use, and relationship. These benefits do not always directly translate objectively into economic value but instead depend on each buyer's subjective assessment.[3]

In business-to-business purchasing, the elements of risk and career consequences come together as an important driver of psychological benefits. The old saying "nobody ever got fired for buying IBM" is an example of this psychological benefit. Buying IBM was considered a safe bet and, therefore, conferred a psychological benefit. Psychological value, as is used in this framework, can include the following:

- Brand
- Risk
- Uncertainty
- Complexity
- Relationship and trust
- Convenience
- Ease of use
- Hassle factors
- Touch and feel
- Sales force knowledge and expertise

Take the example of two companies selling new surgical devices for a new surgical technique. Assume that one company has a highly trained sales force that is perceived as expert in the technology, the surgical technique, and anatomy. Now assume that the other company has a sales force that is perceived as much less competent in all of the same dimensions.

The company with the highly skilled sales force is, all things being equal, bringing greater value to the customer. This company should be able to command a price premium and enjoy a market share advantage. As the new surgical technique matures, this sales force expertise may be less of a factor, but in the earlier stages of the market it is likely to be a source of value.

Value from Whose Perspective?

One of the unique challenges for healthcare suppliers is that the same innovation may create widely divergent value for each of the stakeholders involved in healthcare delivery. For the purposes of this discussion, stakeholders are defined as patients, physicians/caregivers, payers, employers, hospitals, and accountable care organizations. The divergent value is often due to the complexity of payment systems, the timing of changes to reimbursement, and other factors.

At times, an innovation can have negative value for one stakeholder group and significant positive value for others. For example, the first drug-eluting stents approved in the United States brought tremendous value to patents and payers. Yet, there was some indication that US hospitals initially tried to limit their use—due, in part, to the financial impact of the technology on the hospitals.

While there was incremental reimbursement at launch of the technology, the reimbursement only considered the cost of care compared with a bare metal stent procedure. Hospitals feared that coronary artery bypass procedures (CABGs) would be cannibalized by the technology. CABG is a very high-revenue procedure for hospitals.[4]

With the changes to the payment models for providers under healthcare reform, the challenge of selling value becomes even greater. Healthcare suppliers will need to think carefully about where value is created in the healthcare value chain and who benefits. Part of this trick of assessing value is understanding the reimbursement system and its incentives.

Figure 6.4 summarizes key stakeholders and perspectives to consider when quantifying a value proposition for them.

Figure 6.4. Stakeholder value perspectives

	STAKEHOLDER	PERSPECTIVE
Broad ↑ Value Focus ↓ Narrow	Insurer / Health System	Help appropriately manage a population's health and costs
	Accountable Care Organization	Help reduce those costs which are in scope and also help achieve quality goals
	Hospital Level	Help reduce costs, optimize reimbursement, and improve patient satisfaction and outcomes
	Department in Hospital	Help achieve budget goals and performance / quality ratings

QUANTIFY YOUR VALUE TO PROVIDERS

A provider is a hospital, surgical center, laboratory, or other entity that owns the assets where care is delivered. It is important to understand value from this stakeholder's perspective. From the provider's perspective, the basic assessment of value also comes down to two key dimensions—clinical outcomes and financial impact.

This is not to say that product differences such as ease of use, convenience, and other factors do not matter. Many of those differences can be quantified and translated into financial impact.

Financial impact is used since it is broader than costs or TCO. TCO is a common term and means the cost to acquire, operate, maintain, and dispose of a solution. Financial impact is meant to capture the total financial impact of using a technology or intervention, which includes reimbursement. This means it captures both costs and revenues.

Conducting an Initial Value Assessment

Each differentiated benefit of a product or offering could impact multiple elements of value. For example, a new antimicrobial suture that reduces the rate of infection in certain procedures has the potential to impact all elements of value.

Reducing infection rates could improve clinical outcomes, result in lower overall costs due to the use of fewer drugs to treat infections, and provide psychological value to surgeons. The initial value assessment helps to give a big-picture perspective of potential sources of value prior to trying to quantify the value.

Table 6.1 lists potential sources of value for healthcare suppliers. The most promising potential benefits are those that create all three types of value—clinical, economic, and emotional. The individual benefits that impact all three dimensions tend to be clinical. However, they do not have to be restricted to clinical benefits.

For example, a new medical device that is significantly easier to use and that reduces cycle time for a surgical procedure may be viewed initially as a source of economic value. Because the device reduces surgical time, the manufacturer could promote the value of improved OR capacity and scheduling flexibility.

However, it often helps to dig a little deeper. The ease of use of the device could also translate into better clinical outcomes, since the surgeon may not need to work as hard to achieve a successful surgical outcome. It could also impact emotional value, since physicians will benefit from the ease of use. Therefore, something as simple as reducing surgical time could have multiple benefits.

Table 6.1. Initial Value Assessment Checklist

Value element and potential sources of value	Why it matters
Clinical	
Better safety	Improved mortality rate
Improved effectiveness	Fewer repeat procedures or tests, improved patient quality of life (QoL), shorter length of stay, reduced downstream costs
Unmet needs	Addresses area of unmet clinical need
Ease of use	Reduced time to learn and use, potentially better clinical outcomes
Adherence	Improved patient adherence to drug and other therapies
Economic	
Monitoring	Improved monitoring of patients by reducing monitoring costs or reducing adverse events
Maintenance	Reduced non-value-added time spent maintaining equipment or product
Training quality, requirements	Less training needed to educate users to operate the technology or use the device
Quality	Reduced need for rework, testing & inspection, backup
Operating labor required	Fewer resources needed to operate the equipment or prepare the devices and supplies

Value element and potential sources of value	Why it matters
Worker retention	Avoids costs of hiring and training new workers
Worker safety	Reduced lost workdays or other costs related to healthcare workers' workplace safety events
Service needs	More reliable equipment means fewer service visits, fewer spare parts, and less downtime
Cycle time	Solution reduces customer cycle time to complete procedure or diagnostic
Length of stay	Reduce the patient's length of stay within the hospital
Knowledgeable sales force	Sales force helps educate customer on solutions and technology
Inventory management	Able to reduce customers' inventory-related costs
Better service	Faster response, higher-quality service technicians, and more-knowledgeable customer service lowers customer costs or improves uptime
Ordering and shipping	Less time and effort required in ordering and receiving
Access to supplier capabilities	Able to take advantage of supplier capabilities to improve customer business
Acquire and disposal	Lower costs to acquire and dispose of supply or technology
Revenue	Able to help customer grow revenue through increased capacity or to attract new patients
Workflow	Improved workflow or reduced resources needed to deliver care or monitor patients
Downstream costs	Positively impact downstream costs such as repeat procedures, diagnostics, rehab care, nursing home, and readmissions. This is increasingly important for accountable care organizations or providers who are responsible for downstream costs
Reimbursement	Positively impact the customer's reimbursement through better quality, lower costs, or better outcomes. This can include the impact on quality incentives
New technology access	Access to new technology that allows provider to reduce costs or grow

Value element and potential sources of value	Why it matters
Emotional	
Brand	Trust and belief in supplier
Environment	Reduced impact on the environment
Touch and feel	Improved clinician dexterity
Convenience	Improved overall experience with company as a supplier
Relationship	Experience with company and its representatives
Employee engagement	Improved overall healthcare worker employee engagement
Key opinion leader support	Helps provide credibility to the supplier's solution
Quality of clinical evidence	Particularly for new or controversial technologies, the level of clinical evidence is critical in supporting value

Case Study: Safety Needles

Accidental needle sticks from conventional needles are a significant safety issue for healthcare workers. Healthcare workers in the US suffer an estimated 600,000 to 800,000 needle sticks per year.[5] With a host of blood-borne pathogens such as HIV and hepatitis potentially in the dirty needles, hospitals and other healthcare facilities face significant potential costs related to needle sticks. It is estimated that each needle stick costs $3,000 alone in testing and monitoring to determine whether the injured worker has been exposed to a dangerous pathogen.[6]

In response to this significant safety issue, new devices called safety, or retractable, needles were developed. Immediately after use, these devices retract the needle to protect workers from needle sticks. In addition to preventing needle sticks, the technology also reduces disposal costs, since the retracted needles take up much less room in disposal containers.[7]

A quick review of safety needles compared with standard needles leads to the initial value assessment shown in Table 6.2. Five key areas of potential value are identified. Four of the five are related to economic value and should easily be quantified. The fifth area relates to emotional value and, while harder to quantify, offers significant potential leverage.

Table 6.2. Safety Needle Value Assessment

Value element and potential sources of value	Why it matters
Economic	
Training quality, requirements	Less training needed to educate healthcare workers about how to handle unsafe needles
Worker retention	Avoid costs of hiring and training new workers due to fear of being injured
Worker safety	Reduced lost workdays or other costs related to healthcare workers' workplace safety events
Acquire and disposal	Reduced costs of disposing of supply or technology
Emotional	
Employee engagement	Improved overall healthcare worker employee engagement

Quantifying Economic Value to Provider

There are a number of ways to calculate value. Usually, the best approach is to keep things simple. The goal is not to calculate value out to eight decimal places; rather it is to get a starting point that is directionally correct.

One of the simplest ways to begin is to bring together a cross-functional team of people from your organization. They should understand the customer's business model, the disease state, the customer's supply chain, reimbursement, and provider finances. Using a flipchart or whiteboard, go through the following steps.

1. *Identify the next best alternative.* Just about every product or solution has some alternative treatment or diagnostic option. Sometimes the best alternative is to do nothing. You should list the next best

alternative you are comparing your product or solution against. If there are a number of different options, choose the two or three that represent what you will be competing with.

2. *List the differentiated features.* List those features you believe are key and are different from the next best alternative. For a balanced view, these should include features that are better than as well as those that are worse than the next best alternative. One of the signals to a buyer that your value analysis is slanted is not seeing areas where you are worse than the next best alternative. You need to present an objective view of value in order to be credible.

3. *Identify who benefits.* Identify which of the stakeholders involved will benefit or receive value from the technology or solution. A solution may benefit multiple stakeholders. However, it's unlikely that the impact on each stakeholder will be the same. You need to be sure that the value that is quantified is directly translatable to that stakeholder. It should be something they care about. As an example, it may be nice that your technology reduces downstream costs for a private payer. A hospital, however, may not care about this.

4. *Translate features into benefits.* For each differentiated feature, connect it to a need for one or more stakeholders. Write down the benefit in simple terms. In other words, if you had to tell a customer tomorrow, what simple message would you use? For example, if you had a new technology that eliminated the need to repeat procedures or follow-up care, you would need to have a very simple metric for it. You could say that for every 100 patients treated with the technology, you prevent 10 repeat procedures.

5. *Write a value word equation.* Keep it simple. Write out how you would calculate value for each benefit. This is really important. Customers will challenge your assumptions and calculations. This is actually a good sign. You have them debating value and the quantification of value, but not price. Writing out your calculation in simple word equations helps you be transparent about how the data are

calculated. When challenged, the person delivering the value message needs to be able to explain how the numbers were developed.

6. *Quantify the value.* Now apply some simple math to quantify the value. Note the source and precision of each data element. Also, where there is a range for certain data points, consider using a range for the value calculation.

7. *List evidence, assumptions, and sources.* The analysis needs to be credible. Also, it's likely that your legal and regulatory department will not allow you to communicate a value story unless it is substantiated by evidence. You should carefully document the sources of data.

This type of exercise has been done many times with sales teams. I've been highly impressed with the quality of thinking and the results that a sales team can develop in a short exercise. Even if you do not have all the data needed at your fingertips, your sales team can do a reasonably good job of quantifying the value.

Case Study: Patient Ventilator—Economic or Financial Value to Customer Analysis for Hospital

Ventilators are machines that pump oxygen into sick patients' lungs. They cost from $3,000 for basic models to $40,000 for sophisticated models. Like many purchases, especially for equipment, it is important to look at not just the acquisition cost but also the total cost of the various solutions.

Calculating TCO, as the term is used in purchasing, means quantifying differences in the short- and long-term impact of not just the direct purchase price but also all the costs and benefits associated with acquiring and using alternative offerings. For marketers, this should sound very similar to value, or economic value to customers (EVC), or customer financial impact.

In practical terms, estimating EVC or TCO comes down to looking at both the positive and negative differences between your product or solution and the next best alternative. For this simple example of a ventilator, let us assume that there are two suppliers' solutions to compare—Ventilator A and Ventilator B (see Table 6.3).

Assume that both solutions perform roughly the same. Ventilator A has a purchase price of $29,000, and Ventilator B has a price of $34,500, about 19 percent more. However, a closer look at cost of ownership reveals the real value. Ventilator A has filters that need to be changed four times a year. Each filter costs $100. Ventilator B has filters as well, but they only need to be changed once a year and cost about $100 each.

Ventilator A has a flow sensor that needs to be changed at least once over its estimated seven-year life. Ventilator B uses a different technology and will not need to have a sensor changed. Due to its design, Ventilator A will require about $3,000 in annual maintenance costs. Ventilator B, on the other hand, will require about $2,500 in annual maintenance costs. Using these data, one can estimate the TCO for each over a seven-year life.

Table 6.3. Example of Total Cost of Ownership Summary

Cost	Ventilator A	Ventilator B
Acquisition price	$29,000	$34,500
Maintenance (7 years)	$21,000	$17,500
Filters (7 years total)	$2,800	$700
Flow sensor	$900	$0
Total cost of ownership	$53,700	$52,700

Table 6.4 summarizes the total cost of ownership for the two solutions.[8] Although Ventilator A has a much lower purchase price, its higher maintenance and operating costs cause it to have a higher TCO than Ventilator B.

Table 6.4. Ventilator B Compared with Ventilator A

Feature (product facts/data) and benefit (what does it do for customer?)	Value formula (what is the word formula to calculate value?)	Quantified value (what is the quantified value?)	Source/ data
Feature: Filter lasts longer			
Benefit: Requires fewer filters and changes	(Vent. A filter costs/yr) – (Vent. B filter costs/yr) × 7 yrs	$2,800 – $700 = $2,100	Workflow study
Feature: Lower maintenance requirements			
Benefit: Lower costs and less down time	(Vent. A maintenance costs/yr) – (Vent. B maintenance costs/yr) × 7 yrs	$21,000 – $17,500 = $3,500	Estimated
Feature: New flow sensor technology			
Benefit: No need to replace sensor	No. of Vent. A sensor changes over equipment life × cost/sensor	1 × $900 = $900	Estimated

Calculating potential value in a structured way is critical. Table 6.4 shows a simple framework for translating features and benefits into quantifiable value. The table is completed from the perspective of Ventilator B's company.

In this example, each of the features is translated into one or more benefits. Here, for example, the feature of filters lasting longer translates into significant value for Ventilator B's company. In summary, there appears to be $6,500 in total value created, compared with Ventilator A. So, in theory, a price difference of less than $6,500 would mean Company B would provide more value or a lower TCO.

This is a simplistic example. In practice, the supplier would need to consider whether to discount economic benefits that occur over time in terms of present value. This would allow for an apples-to-apples comparison with the acquisition costs. Another consideration would be to review the variables and assumptions around value. It is likely that certain segments of hospitals get a much bigger benefit than other segments. Finally, the medical technology company would need to consider how much of the value to share with the customer to induce purchase.

CONNECT YOUR VALUE TO BUSINESS MODELS

Connect Value to New Reimbursement Models

Anyone who has worked in healthcare for any length of time knows that the reimbursement and payment rules constantly change. In the US, each year the Centers for Medicare and Medicaid Services (CMS) refines existing and defines new rules for both inpatient and outpatient payment and rates. Rather than address specific elements of healthcare reform, I provide a framework for thinking about your value as it relates to the providers' business and payment model.

In the past in the United States, providers were paid based on a fee-for-service model. The provider performed a service, and they were paid for that service. For example, a hospital would perform a coronary stenting procedure, and they were paid for that procedure.

This fee-for-service payment model was loaded with many perverse incentives and lacked a connection to value. The more of an activity a hospital performed, the more it was paid. Furthermore, there was no connection to quality of care or outcomes. So, a hospital with outstanding outcomes was paid the same as a hospital with poor outcomes. All of this is changing under the healthcare reform known as the Affordable Care Act (ACA).

Under the ACA, there are a number of areas to consider as you try to quantify your value. This has added some complexity to the value quantification, but it also opens up new ways to create value for your customers. What follows is a high-level explanation of these programs. You should be looking for opportunities to create value for your customer under these programs. In general, there are four areas to consider when quantifying your value.

- *Value-based purchasing.* CMS has implemented a number of new programs to reward providers for improving quality of care and outcomes. These include patient satisfaction measures, process of care measures, outcomes measures, and efficiency measures. The specific reimbursement penalty or bonus for value-based purchasing is based on a "total performance score" that is calculated based on a combination of these measures.[9] This is a mandatory program that US acute care hospitals participate in.

- *Quality programs.* CMS has implemented programs focused on penalizing or rewarding hospitals for quality. As of this writing, there are two such programs. One is the hospital acquired conditions (HAC) program. In this program, hospitals are rewarded or penalized for the rate of preventable events or accidents. The other program is readmission penalties. Under the readmission reduction program, hospitals are rewarded or penalized for the rate of readmissions related to certain diagnoses.[10] This is a mandatory program that US hospitals participate in.

- *Accountable care organizations (ACOs).* ACOs are a new mechanism for CMS to reward providers who come together to coordinate care. The goal is to reduce costs and improve care through better coordination of care. The ACO is accountable for a patient over a three-year period. This includes the cost for inpatient and outpatient care. The ACOs must achieve a level of performance on a set of quality measures. ACOs are a voluntary program, and providers are not required to participate. See Appendix B for more details on the ACO program.

- *Bundled payments.* This is a pilot program whereby a hospital and physician receive one "bundled" payment. Under the existing reimbursement system, the hospital and physicians each receive a separate payment for delivering care. The bundled payment is meant to encourage coordination of care and alignment of incentives between the physician and hospital. Several different models are being piloted.[11]

Many providers are struggling to understand and manage these new programs introduced through healthcare reform. For a supplier, these programs represent a potential opportunity to find areas where your solution provides unique value. Table 6.5 provides a simple framework for organizing your value proposition. The impact of your solution is likely to vary from customer to customer since each customer will be in a different situation.

Table 6.5. Connect Your Value to Customer Reimbursement Model

Reimbursement program	What opportunities do you see?	Insights or data for the customer . . .	Questions to lead with . . .
Quality programs			
Value-based purchasing			
Bundled payments			
ACOs			

For example, let's say you were introducing a new device that reduced heart failure readmissions. Heart failure readmissions are among the diagnoses included in the 30-day readmission reduction program. Hospitals that have excessive readmissions related to heart failure can be penalized under this program. If your device reduces readmission, there may be an opportunity to quantify what that reduction in readmission translates to in terms of a reduced penalty to the hospitals.

Connect Value to Provider Business Model

As the market evolves, the provider business models are changing as well. Many providers in the US now own or have started their own insurance plans. These plans could be for just their own employees or these could be insurance products that the providers sell to employers and others. In this case, quantifying your value proposition has another level of complexity.

In general, you'll need to consider what services and time horizon the insurance plan covers. The provider may be at risk for managing the total patient costs over a longer period than for just an acute care visit. In this case, you will want to carefully consider the impact of your solution on the downstream costs outside of the acute care setting and quantify any savings relative to the next best alternative.

KEY TAKEAWAYS

- Understanding value is the foundation of selling in the new market.

- Companies must move away from a focus on features and benefits to a focus on value.

- Value has three dimensions—clinical, economic, and emotional. Although emotional value is real and should be considered, economic and clinical value are the foundation of the value equation.

- For healthcare suppliers, stakeholders are increasingly using economic and clinical value to make buying decisions, so it is important that suppliers themselves understand the value their solutions bring.

- Suppliers will also need to be able to quantify the impact of their solutions on the customers' reimbursement and business model.

NOTES

1. www.brainyquote.com (accessed February 7, 2014).

2. A. All, "Procurement Must Look Beyond 'Stuff' to Strategy," *IT Business Edge,* July 2007 (accessed January 16, 2010).

3. T. Levitt, *Industrial Purchasing Behavior: A Study of Communication Effects* (Division of Research, Graduate School of Business Administration, Harvard University, 1965); and T. T. Nagle and J. E. Hogan, *The Strategy and Tactics of Pricing: A Guide to Growing Profitably* (4th ed.) (Upper Saddle River, NJ: Prentice Hall, 2006).

4. J. Hodgson et al., "Drug-Eluting Stent Task Force: Final Report and Recommendations of the Working Committees on Cost-Economics, Access to Care, and Medicolegal Issues," *Catheterization and Cardiovascular Interventions* 62 (2004): 1–17.

5. National Institute for Occupational Safety and Health (NIOSH), "Safer Medical Device Implementation in Health Care Facilities: Sharing Lessons Learned," www.cdc.gov/niosh/topics/bbp/safer/ (accessed September 6, 2004).

6. I. Hatcher, "Reducing Sharps Injuries Among Health Care Workers: A Sharps Container Quality Improvement Project," *The Joint Commission Journal on Quality Improvement* 28.9 (July 2004).

7. See vanishpoint.com (accessed June 28, 2012).

8. J. Herbert, "Total Cost of Ownership on Hospital Equipment," *South African Federation of Hospital Engineering,* March 2003 (accessed January 17, 2011).

9. See CMS.gov.

10. Ibid.

11. Ibid.

Chapter | 7

CREATE FLEXIBLE OFFERS AND TRADES

To the man who only has a hammer, everything he encounters begins to look like a nail.

—Abraham Maslow[1]

If you've purchased a car recently, you likely had many decisions to make. These included what model to buy, which color, and which of the various option packages to select. All of these choices represent ways that the car manufacturers can vary the physical product to meet the needs of different consumers.

When buying the car, you had other things to consider as well. These include items like the warranty, service, and financing. A standard warranty is included with a car purchase, but you can also buy extended coverage for an additional fee. Likewise, some auto manufacturers bundle in free routine maintenance. Other companies charge separately for routine service. You had to decide whether to lease, purchase outright, or finance the car. Finally, you had to decide how much to spend.

At a basic level, an offering is the combination of the product, services, business terms, and price that you agree to with a customer. As consumers, we encounter businesses using offering strategies all the time. Whether the transaction involves a car, movie tickets, or a seat on an airplane, companies selling to consumers use flexible offers to vary the value delivered and charge different prices to meet the needs of different customers.

How does this relate to healthcare? If you sell to hospitals or other healthcare providers, do all of your customers have the same needs? Do they all value your products, services, and support in the same way? Are their budgets exactly the same? If you answered "no" to any of these questions, then you need some flexibility in your offering.

There's another key reason to have flexible offers and trades when selling to providers. Both of these are powerful tools for negotiating with tough buyers. In this chapter, we'll explore creating flexible offers and trades for healthcare suppliers.

KEY COMPONENTS OF FLEXIBLE OFFERINGS

In the car example above, the auto dealer could vary many different parts of the offering, including the physical product, services, and financing. In healthcare, it's helpful to think about your offering in terms of four categories: the core product/service solution, enabling technologies, services, and business terms. Figure 7.1 illustrates the various parts of the offering.

Figure 7.1. Components of the offering

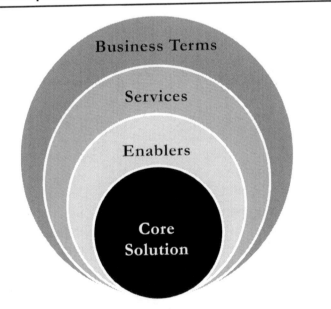

Offering Part 1: Core Product or Service Solution

The core product or service is the primary item you sell. If you were selling interventional cardiology products, then your core product would be items like stents and balloons. If you were a clinical laboratory, then your core service would be the testing service or diagnostic results. For a pharmaceutical company, it would be the drug.

You may offer different versions of the same product. For example, a clinical laboratory might offer multiple diagnostics that test for the same thing, but at a different quality level or specificity—for example, a basic cholesterol test and a more advanced lipids test. However, both of these would be considered the core product. Figure 7.2 provides examples of core products/services.

Figure 7.2. Examples of core products/services

Market	Core Product	Enabler
Clinical laboratory	• Clinical chemistry and immunoassay instrument	• Remote monitoring • Sample storage & retrieval
Interventional cardiology	• Drug-eluting stent	• Delivery system
Orthopaedics	• Implant	• Instrument kit
Radiology	• CT Scan	• Specialized workflow or image management software
General surgery	• Single-use devices	• Pre-packaged procedure kits
Pharmaceutical	• Vial of new drug	• Companion diagnostic

Offering Part 2: Enabling Technologies

An enabling technology is something used in conjunction with the core product. One way to think about enabling technologies is that they often help to magnify or enhance the value of the core technology. They help, for example, perform a procedure or achieve a diagnostic result better, faster, or cheaper. When the core product matures, often the real value difference between suppliers is created in the enabling technologies. Examples of enabling technologies include these:

- Delivery systems for implantable products

- Automation in the clinical diagnostics market

- Informatics that connect your solution to the hospital information system

- Procedure or instrument kits that are used with implants

- New imaging technologies that allow the physician to get a better result during a procedure

- Companion diagnostic for a new drug

- Remote monitoring system

If your core product matures, and the buyer uses the typical line "all these technologies are the same—it now comes down to price," look at your enabling technologies. It might be true that the core technologies offer similar outcomes and performance. Yet, you might have a big advantage in the enabling technology you sell. This is when you need to make sure that the core product is not bundled together with the enabling technology. Unbundling and charging separately for the core product and enabling technology may be a way to fight off a buyer's commoditization attack.

Offering Part 3: Services

The other component of the offering is the surrounding services provided by the supplier. In the healthcare industry, many suppliers have tried to compete by adding value-added services. Over time, the number of services that are provided for free or bundled into the price of the core product becomes overwhelming. Often, these services are highly valuable and could make great trades.

In the healthcare industry, a number of services can be offered:

- Customer training
- Break fix service (service hours, response time, etc.)
- Delivery time
- Shipment frequency
- Telephone support
- Spare parts
- Process improvement
- Special consulting
- Consigning inventory
- Inventory management
- Customer start-up
- Technical support
- Co-development
- Clinical support
- Clinical centers of excellence
- Priority access to new technologies

Obviously, a number of these are critical to appropriate use of the product for clinical care. As an example, a company selling a new digital pathology solution to a hospital laboratory will need to train the staff to use the technology. The question is not whether the company offers training but how much training it offers, and whether it offers the same level of training to a very large customer who purchases a million dollars' worth of equipment and a customer who purchases a hundred thousand dollars' worth of equipment.

Offering Part 4: Business Terms

Finally, another way to vary the offering in order to provide negotiation flexibility and create trades is to look at the business terms that are offered. Business terms govern how you and the customer will do business together. These often have a significant impact on customer profitability:

- Payment terms
- Financing
- Contract length
- Cancellation fees
- Purchase commitments
- Bundles purchased
- Legal terms
- Risk-sharing arrangements
- Number of suppliers on agreement
- Supplier status—primary or secondary
- Priority of your solution in patient treatment—first line or second therapy
- Priority of test in diagnosis—screening or confirmatory test
- Patient co-payment amount

In total, there are four broad levers that can be used to adapt the offering. These are the core product, enabling technologies, services, and the business terms that surround the deal. Each part of the offering can be thought of as a trade.

A trade is simply something that can be used to provide or receive value during negotiations. For example, your delivery terms could be something that is a trade. Your standard terms may be to deliver once a week. However, if the customer wants a lower price, maybe you could move to delivery once a month. This would lower your costs, and allow you to pass on the lower costs to the customer.

UNCOVERING YOUR TRADES

Unfortunately, if your company hasn't put a lot of thought into it, you are likely to have a bit of a mess in terms of the offerings and trades that are used with customers. Usually, it is a small group of clever salespeople who figure out what to offer to various customers and the trades to use during negotiations. Rather than do this one-off for each customer, it's best to give structure and create guidelines for the trades and offerings to be used.

This is a simple exercise that could be completed in an afternoon. It's best done with a cross-functional team that includes people who have different touch points with the customer. They could be from sales, marketing, finance, supply chain, customer service, and other areas. The goal is to identify all of the potential trades that can be used with customers. Once the trades are identified, you can combine them into some logical offerings. Let's start by identifying the trades.

Gather your cross-functional team. On a flipchart, draw Figure 7.3. In the first column, list the offering or key product you are evaluating. In the second column, list all the ways you can vary what you provide to the customer. Think about the four offering parts we discussed above.

Figure 7.3. Trade identification template

Offering or Product Line	Potential "Trade"	Value to Customer	Cost to You

In the next column, list the value to the customer. If you can't quantify the value at this point, just list the benefits for now. In the last column, you should try to get some general sense of the cost to you. In other words, what it costs you to provide this trade to the customer. At this point, you should be trying to get a rough idea. As you perform this exercise, consider all services that are currently provided to the customer. These could be free services, charged services, and services that are bundled into the product price.

An example of a list of trades for a digital pathology system might look like Table 7.1. For simplicity's sake, the value to the customer is listed in terms of benefits. If this were a real situation, you would want to quantify the benefits.

Table 7.1. Example of Trades for Digital Pathology System

Potential "trades"	Value to customer	Cost to you
Basic break fix service (business hours)	Basic service to fix the instrument and get it back and running—4-hour guaranteed response time	Average $12,000 per year per instrument
24×7 service agreement	Customer is guaranteed instrument uptime. Provide 1-hour response time 24 hours × 7 days a week	Average $24,000 per year per instrument
Basic training	Provide basic onsite training up to 12 hours	Average $6,000 per account
Extended training	Provide special training	Average $8,000 per account
Sample storage system	Automated storage and retrieval of samples reduces time and cost of retrieving samples for additional analysis	$56,000 per account
Workflow redesign service	Redesign customer testing workflow to reduce labor costs	$25,000 per account
Basic warranty	1-year warranty for parts and labor	$4,000 per instrument

Potential "trades"	Value to customer	Cost to you
Extended warranty	5-year warranty covers parts and labor	$22,000 per instrument
Normal throughput model	Can handle testing volume needs of most hospitals	N/A
High-throughput model	Hospitals that have higher volume or that need quicker turnaround time. Eliminate the need to send out test to third party, which is very costly	N/A
Advanced image management software	Software allows for quick analysis and comparison of samples. Reduces physician time	N/A

DESIGN AN OFFERING STRATEGY

Designing the Offerings

After you identify all of the potential trades, much like in Table 7.1, you can use these to construct flexible offerings.[2] It's helpful to come up with some basic "standard" offerings of varying value and price to provide to customers. Using the trades from Table 7.1, I've constructed the three standard offerings shown in Figure 7.4.

Each of the offerings in Figure 7.4 provides a different value at a different price. In this case, each offering targets customers with different needs, budgets, and willingness to pay. Customers who want all of the services and the higher performance product can select the higher priced offering. Those who can't afford or don't want to pay for extras can select the good offering.

If you are in the middle of a negotiation with a tough buyer, trades allow you to alter the offering and change the price. If the customer pushes for a lower price, you should be willing to take something away if you decide to lower the price. This is why understanding the value of the trades is important. Likewise, if the buyer is playing games with you, one strategy is to present multiple offers. You could provide a higher priced, higher value offer as well as a lower priced, lower value offer.

Figure 7.4. Example of offering strategy

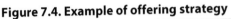

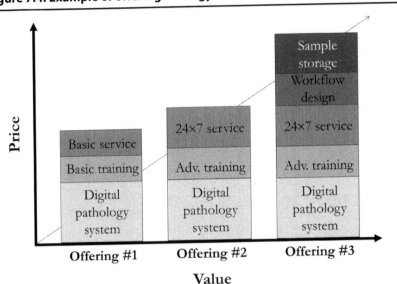

One of the simplest tricks professional buyers use is to pull you into a bidding war with other suppliers. As one professional buyer said, "I always try to create a price war with my vendors; it usually works."[3] The other simple trick is to try to convince you that your solution is identical to everyone else's. As one professional buyer said in an interview, "I pick out what supplier I want in advance. It is usually the higher price, higher value supplier. I then include lots of competitors in the bid to get the higher value supplier's price down."[4]

Rather than play this game, you can use flexible offers to lower the price without devaluing your high-value offering. There's another advantage of the offering strategy. If you are dealing with an account where you think the users have a different need from the professional buyers, presenting multiple offers with different prices and value can help uncover this.

Name the Relationship

Another strategic use of offerings during selling and negotiations is to be explicit about the type of relationship the buyer is asking for. It often helps to "label" each of the offerings. For example, the basic low-cost offering could be called a "transactional relationship." The high-end offering could be called a "strategic relationship."

As a supplier, you don't have unlimited resources. You must choose which customers to invest in and what types of relationships you want to have. Likewise, buyers can't have strategic relationships with every supplier. Not every supplier is strategic. The buyer must make choices as well about the type of suppliers it seeks to create a strategic relationship with.

By naming the relationship, you are being explicit about the products, services, and support you are providing at different price points. You are also being explicit that customers who want low prices only are transactional customers. There's nothing wrong with having a transactional relationship as long as both sides understand the costs and benefits of this. You are simply being explicit about it.

For example, you may have a deep pipeline of new products. For some of these products, you may not be able to supply or train the entire market during the initial launch period. Do you want to provide priority access for these products to transactional customers? You probably want to provide access to customers who have a long-term strategic relationship with you.

As healthcare buyers become more sophisticated, your ability to be explicit about your relationships becomes more important. Professional buyers in other industries usually have more experience with supplier relationship management (SRM). SRM is basically a process for buyers to manage supplier relationships strategically. This includes systematic collaboration to improve performance for the customer and the supplier.[5] As the provider supply chain matures, SRM will be more important for them.

Your ability to be explicit with the customer about the type of relationship and the offerings for each will help you clarify your strategy. It will also help the customer make choices. If your customer is still relatively immature from a supply chain perspective, you will be helping to educate them. If they are more mature, they will appreciate your honesty and thoughtfulness. If they are playing games with you, you have a way to call their bluff. I talk more about this in later chapters.

KEY TAKEAWAYS

- Flexible offerings and trades are ways to vary the value delivered to the customer along with the price.

- Trades and offers are key tools that help during the sales and negotiation process.

- Offerings and trades should be developed on purpose; they should not just evolve over time. Companies lacking a purposeful approach and clear rules and policies can easily create a messy situation.

- Developing multiple offers and naming them are ways to be explicit to the buyer about the type of relationship that each offer is intended for.

NOTES

1. www.ThinkExist.com (accessed December 2, 2013).

2. Adapted from J. Anderson and J. Narus, *Flexible Market Offerings: Naked Solutions, With Options* (Institute for the Study of Business Markets, Pennsylvania State University, February 18, 1994).

3. C Provines, "Professional Buyers' View of Suppliers" (Unpublished manuscript, 2013).

4. Ibid.

5. C. Dominick and S. Lunney, *The Procurement Game Plan* (J. Ross Publishing, 2012).

Chapter | 8

IDENTIFY AND LEVERAGE BUYING BEHAVIORS

If there is any one secret of success, it lies in the ability to get the other person's point of view and see things from that person's angle as well as from your own.

—Henry Ford[1]

Just like consumers, organizations tend to have an identifiable buying behavior. Think about customers you call on or know. Some may be very formal and follow rigid processes, even for seemingly small purchases like office supplies. Others may be much less formal. Beyond the formality of the purchasing process, there are other clues that accounts have different buying behaviors.

As a result of their mission or competitive situation, some accounts are extremely interested in innovation. They want to be on the cutting edge and are willing to pay for it. These are usually academic medical centers. Other accounts seem much more price sensitive. It may seem like every nickel they have to spend is their last.

Likewise, some providers want piles of data before they will make a buying decision. This includes clinical and economic data. It may seem like they never have enough data. Alternatively, some accounts are more relationship oriented. It's the long-term relationship, not the data, that builds trust. All of these are clues to buying behavior. Understanding what clues to look for will help you categorize your customers by buying behavior.

Why bother identifying your accounts' buying behaviors? Customers with different buying behaviors often want different things from their suppliers. Their different buying behaviors will also dictate how they engage with suppliers and what information they need to make a buying decision. In addition, they usually treat suppliers differently. Some view suppliers as costs only. Other customers view suppliers as assets. Properly identifying your customers' buying behaviors will allow you to propose the right offerings, provide the correct information, and prepare for negotiations. This chapter is focused on identifying and leveraging buying behavior.

DRIVERS OF BUYING BEHAVIOR

Figure 8.1. Drivers of buying behavior

There are five key drivers of buying behaviors. These factors impact how the organization procures goods and services and influence their focus on costs, value, risk, collaboration, and other factors in the purchasing equation. Based on research and experience, I detail the five factors affecting healthcare organizational buying behaviors below and summarize them in Figure 8.1.

Driver 1—Financial Situation

The customer's financial situation will drive their buying behavior. Customers in relatively difficult situations will tend to base decisions more on price and less on value. For example, a hospital facing a financial crisis may behave very differently than a growing hospital with a healthy payer mix. If you sell the same product or service to these two customers, their differing financial situations will drive different buying behaviors. Their respective financial situations could also impact their willingness to invest in goods or services with a longer-term payoff.

Driver 2—The Organization's Goals/Strategies

The goals and strategies of the organization as a whole often dictate how they treat suppliers and buy goods and services. Customers operating in highly competitive markets may be more interested in new technologies or new profitable businesses. Innovation may be critical to them. On the other hand, a customer facing a short-term turnaround or restructuring may be interested in immediate cost savings. The organization's overall goals and strategies are often, but not always, translated into a procurement or sourcing strategy. It's important that you understand your customer's overall goals, since these will usually influence their buying behavior.

Driver 3—Supply Chain Structure and Maturity

The structure and maturity of the professional buying organization in the company will drive buying behavior. More mature, sophisticated organizations take a broader view of value and are willing to consider value in the buying decision. More mature organizations also tend to view the supplier network more strategically. This does not mean they will not test and push you in negotiations. It simply means that relative to a less-sophisticated buyer organization, they will be more value oriented and willing to consider other ways of joint value creation. On the other hand, less-sophisticated organizations will tend to be more focused on costs, and often price, only. The structure of the procurement or materials management organization will also influence how it buys.

Driver 4—Organizational Buying Rules and Process

Some organizations follow specific rules and requirements for procuring goods and services. This is particularly true for government-related organizations. Sometimes they are required to choose the lowest bidder. Other organizations may have implemented formal policies for buying such as multiple bid requirements for certain levels of spend. Pay close attention to the buying rules or to any recent changes in the customer's buying rules.

Driver 5—Hospital–Physician Relationship

The relationship between the physicians and the hospital also plays a critical role in how the organization buys. In the US, there has been a shift in the number of physicians who are employed by hospitals. Depending on which projection you look at, it is estimated that 50 to 75% of physicians will be employed by hospitals in the future.[2] This, of course, will differ by region and specialty.[3] The bottom line is that the physician's ties to and influence on the hospital will impact how much influence they have in the purchasing decision. It will also influence how aligned they are with the financial interests of the hospital.

BUYING BEHAVIOR IS NOT STATIC

Although a customer may procure goods and services the same way for years, their process can suddenly change. This is usually a signal or clue that something is going on. For example, you may have been selling to the user of a service for many years. Suddenly, you're told by your key contact that they need to send the business out to bid. This could be a negotiation ploy, or it could signal a change.

The following story highlights the risk of changing buying behavior. A salesperson for a particular supplier had a long and tight relationship with the key decision maker, who happened to be the department head. The decision maker never wanted to even discuss sending this particular purchase out to bid. Even after smart purchasing people presented compelling analysis showing huge savings opportunities in this particular spend area, the department head refused to go out to bid.

The next year, due to financial issues, the account had to initiate severe budget cuts in all areas. Purchasing was held out as a tool to help achieve the budget cuts. Department heads were told to either start cutting supplier costs or start firing people. You can probably guess what happened next.

Suddenly, the long-term relationship really wasn't that important. It's much easier to squeeze a supplier than to start firing people. The department head sent the business out to bid. Even though the company stayed with the incumbent vendor, it got a substantial price reduction.

What happened to the relationship? After the incumbent supplier substantially reduced its price, everyone involved in the buying decision started to wonder whether they had been taken advantage of all those years. They never trusted that supplier again. It's an important reminder that there are factors that can cause a customer to change its buying behavior. When buying behavior starts to change, you need to be ready!

FOUR KEY BUYER BEHAVIOR TYPES

Identifying buying behavior is not an academic or abstract exercise. This should be a real tool to help you sell better and waste less time in the sales process. From a value selling perspective, it should also help you get clear about what offerings to present to which customers. Finally, from a negotiations point of view, it will help you match your negotiation strategy to the needs and buying behavior of your customer.

There are many different models of buying behavior. The goal here is to present a generic model that fits hospitals and healthcare buyers. Some healthcare suppliers have customer segmentation models with three key segments. Other healthcare suppliers have models with five segments. The point is that you should have some way of identifying the underlying buying behavior of the account. If you already have a model, use it. Moreover, you should use this understanding of their buying behavior to win more deals at prices that make sense.

There are four buying behavior types, presented below.[4] For each type, there are "clues" to identifying this buyer type along with strategies to consider for each buying behavior. Figure 8.2 summarizes the four buyer behavior segments. A detailed description is provided below.

Figure 8.2. Buyer behavior segments

Value Seeker	Traditional (relationship) Buyer	Innovator	Price Buyer
• Often called a "big picture" buyer • Considers clinical & economic value • Usually sophisticated buyer with committee buying process • Willing to make trade-offs • Will work with vendor to achieve its cost and quality goals	• Usually an account where physicians still have power • Could be a rural or small hospital • Relies heavily on supplier for expertise, training, support, and advice	• Innovation focused • May be referral center • Quality, outcomes, and data focused • Advancing the science is important	• Really cares primarily about price or acquisition costs • Not interested in TCO • Can be under financial pressure, short-sighted • Buying decisions often driven by economic buyer

Value Seeker

This customer sees the big picture. They consider both clinical and economic value. They are usually a sophisticated buyer with a committee buying process. They are willing to work with vendors and will make trade-offs. Often, they will consider switching for better value. However, always remember that it is much easier to reduce the incumbent vendor's prices than to switch vendors.

In response to the changes to the healthcare system in the US, this type of account is becoming increasingly dominant. The reimbursement system and the changing landscape are pushing hospitals to focus on value. Value is not just about lower prices. It's about quality, patient outcomes, and patient satisfaction.

What Are the Clues?

These customers want value. But this doesn't mean they can always quantify value. You must connect the dots for them. In healthcare, a value assessment is a balanced view of clinical and economic perspectives. Therefore, this buyer, more than any other, will likely have a committee buying process that balances the perspectives of clinicians and others. Specific clues include these:

- Formal buying process
- Value analysis committee or other buying committees
- Some history of physician and hospital administration collaboration
- Usually a sophisticated buyer
- Data-driven, looking for both clinical and economic data

Traditional (Relationship) Buyer

This is the old, traditional hospital buyer. It is an account where the physicians still significantly influence product selection and make many of the buying decisions with little influence from administration. The account relies on suppliers for expertise and support. Relationships are important here. This is usually the favorite type of account for salespeople who rely primarily on relationship and clinical selling. Unfortunately, it is also the type of buyer that is shrinking over time.

About 20 years ago, this was the buying behavior at many hospitals. Over time, with changes in the marketplace and with the new payment models, this buyer type is quickly disappearing. The trend of physicians moving from private practice to employed hospital staff is also driving this shift. Here are some clues to consider.

What Are the Clues?

- Buying decision is driven primarily by physician or clinician
- Physicians are less likely to be employed by the hospital
- Usually, less formal buying process
- Materials management has little influence
- The customer looks to the vendor for expertise and support
- Can be a follower or late follower from a new technology adoption perspective
- Tends to be less price sensitive
- Can be a small, isolated or rural hospital

Innovator

This is usually a large academic-affiliated hospital. It can be a referral center and is usually involved in advancing the science. Quality, outcomes, and advancing the science are all critical for these types of hospitals. These customers are willing to switch for access to new innovation.

What Are the Clues?

- Larger, much more sophisticated accounts
- Innovators and early adopters of new technologies
- Often committee buying process
- Focused on cutting-edge technology and care for many service lines
- Often involved in clinical trials
- More data and evidence driven than other buying types

Price-Cost Buyer

This buyer is focused on the price or cost of the supply. They tend to be extremely price sensitive. They generally don't understand or don't care about total value. Their behavior could be due to extreme financial pressure, the people involved in buying, or other situational factors.

Unfortunately, many salespeople easily misread professional buyers' negotiation tactics and assume that the customer is a price buyer. As mentioned, professional buyers are paid to take costs out. They employ a variety of tactics to achieve this goal. One of these is to focus heavily on price and try to convince you that the decision is all about price.

So, don't mistake professional buyer tactics with the true underlying buying behavior of the account. Look at the past history of buying. Ask yourself these questions: Do they ever switch incumbent vendors? Do they always make a decision purely based on price? How involved are the clinicians in the buying process?

Look for a pattern and willingness to switch vendors. They often treat suppliers poorly and see suppliers as sources of costs rather as sources of capabilities.

What Are the Clues?

- Frequent requests for proposals (RFPs)
- Likes to test the market
- Invites many suppliers to bid
- Willing to switch suppliers for small price savings
- Administration or materials management driving buying decision
- Not data-driven
- Late adopter of technology
- Not interested in, or highly skeptical of, value stories

ALIGN YOUR TACTICS WITH BUYING BEHAVIOR

Once you identify the buying behavior of your customers, you need to put these insights to work. This is when it's helpful to align your offerings strategy and negotiation tactics with the buyer behavior type. Below are some suggested tactics to use with each type. This is not an exhaustive list. You should spend some time thinking about the solutions you sell and develop tactics specific to your business.

Tactics to Use with Value Seekers

By definition, these customers are interested in value. Therefore, the key with this buyer is to understand their needs and your unique, differentiated value. You should also be prepared to trade value. Specific strategies include these:

1. *Use a credible and convincing value story.* This means quantifying your value and connecting it to the customer's business and payment model.

2. *Prepare multiple offers of varying value.* This can be a "good," "better," and "best" offering set with different prices. This forces choice. It also gives you a way to blunt the tactics of professional buyers who

claim to only care about price. If price is all they care about, offer them a low-priced "good" offering. If, however, they want your top-of-the-line product with all of the relevant services, they will have to pay for it.

3. *Develop a list of trades.* You should prepare in advance a list of trades that can be used to add or take value out of the deal. When pushed for a lower price, the answer shouldn't be yes or no. It should be a conditional "if-then" statement. For example: "If you (Mr. Customer) will agree to commit 60% market share for my three product lines, then I would be willing to provide a better discount."

4. *Track your value and use it in business reviews.* If you are the incumbent or become the incumbent, always remember to track the value you are delivering to the customer. Customers easily forget or try to not recognize the value you bring. Suppliers themselves often forget all the value they bring to customers. This can include training, expedited shipping, co-marketing, priority access to new technologies, and other items. You should incorporate your value into regular business reviews with the customer. If it's an important customer, think about developing a scorecard to use during business reviews. This should include all the value you bring, along with your performance related to delivery, service, training, and support. For sophisticated buyers, supplier scorecards are not new. If you do this right, this will help reinforce your value and create psychological switching barriers (this assumes that you have good value and customer support metrics).

Tactics to Use with Traditional Buyers

Traditional buyers are accounts where the clinicians wield most of the buying influence. Therefore, building relationships with them, supporting their needs, and focusing on the clinical part of selling are critical. Remember that buying behavior often changes. In fact, the buyer type most likely to disappear in the future is the traditional buyer. Specific strategies for this buyer type include the following:

1. *Focus on making the clinicians' life easier.* This could be through the administrative support you provide, the unique solutions your company provides, or your own personal efforts. The focus here is on removing any hassle factors and being seen as a critical partner in helping them.

2. *Demonstrate how your solution helps clinicians' practice.* Focus on clinical outcomes and the impact on the physicians' reputation and own practice. This could also include unique training and education that your company provides.

3. *Find ways to continually add value.* For the account itself, search for ways to continually add value and create stickiness. This could be through training, reimbursement support, extra supply-chain services, or other ways of adding value to the account. Obviously, these should be things that make good business sense and that fall within your company's rules and guidelines.

4. *Build lasting relationships.* Since this buying behavior tends to be less formal and businesslike, relationships are important. You should find ways to build relationships with many members of the account, not just the clinicians.

Tactics to Use with Innovators

Because of their competitive strategy and focus, innovators are interested in new innovations, and in advancing the science. Your tactics need to clearly align with this. Specific tactics for this buyer type include these:

1. *Highlight innovation capabilities.* These customers want to know that their suppliers will help them differentiate themselves. Therefore, your pipeline and innovation capabilities are critical.

2. *Demonstrate value of innovation.* While innovation is the focus with this type of customer, it is usually not innovation for innovation's sake. This customer seeks to differentiate themselves competitively and to create value. Therefore, you should help them connect the dots on value. This means translating what the value of your innovation actually means to their business.

3. *Focus on the science.* These accounts are typically involved in clinical trials and deeply focused on helping advance the science. You should be prepared to discuss outcomes and quality of innovations.

4. *Develop the right trades.* Trades are tools for negotiating and defending value. Not every customer will value all of your potential trades the same way. In the case of the innovator, obviously, your trades related to innovation are critical. This could include priority access to new technologies, for example.

Tactics to Use with Price-Cost Buyers

Since these buyers only really care about price or supply costs, they can't or won't see the value of your solution. If you have valuable offerings, this is the worst type of customer to deal with. Many salespeople enjoy working with people and building relationships. They also work hard to try to solve customers' needs. However, with this type of buyer, you are really wasting your time.

1. *Present low-cost, no-frills offering.* For the price buyer, develop a low-cost, low-value offering. When asked for a lower price, offer this.

2. *Don't waste time discussing value.* By definition, this buyer type only cares about price or supply cost. They usually are not interested in ways that you create value for them, either in the hospital, or through lower reimbursement penalties, or any other way.

3. *Establish a clear walk-away.* This is true of negotiating value with any buyer type. You should always have a walk-away defined. However,

it is even more important with this buyer type. Seek alignment within your company on when you will walk away from the deal.

4. *Call out the relationship.* This is one of the tactics you can use to flush out someone acting like a price buyer. For example, when you present your offer, name it. You could say, "This is our offering for transactional customers." A transactional relationship is one where we both agree that there is little value to either side in building a long-term partnership. We agree to do business on terms that make sense.

5. *Present multiple offers.* This is related to number 4 above. If the account is acting like a price buyer and you are uncertain of their true behavior, you could present multiple offers, of varying value. Offer 1 could be a "strategic relationship." This would include services and your best or better product. Offer 2 would be a "transactional relationship." This would include no-frills services and a good-enough product. Your goal is to force the customer to be explicit about the type of relationship they want. As an example, many companies have innovative, new technologies that they will be launching in the future. Priority launch access to these new technologies should not be given to transactional customers.

KEY TAKEAWAYS

- Buying behavior is a way to describe how an account buys goods and services.

- Not all organizations purchase in the same way or exhibit the same behaviors and attitudes towards suppliers.

- Five factors drive buying behavior for a customer. Understanding these factors will provide insights into potential changes in buying behavior.

- When a customer changes its buying behavior, suppliers need to change their selling and negotiation strategy.

- Understanding buying behavior is critical, since it will help you be more efficient and effective in selling and defending value.

- Once you identify and categorize your customers' buying behavior, then you need to create the right tactics to deal with each behavior type.

NOTE

1. www.brainyquote.com (accessed February 7, 2014).

2. See Accenture, "Clinical Transformation: New Business Models for a New Era in Healthcare" (Chicago: Accenture, 2012) (accessed September 4, 2013); and Carol K. Kane and David W. Emmons, "New Data On Physician Practice Arrangements: Private Practice Remains Strong Despite Shifts Toward Hospital Employment," www.ama-assn.org (accessed January 2, 2014).

3. Carol K. Kane and David W. Emmons, "New Data On Physician Practice Arrangements."

4. There are many different types of segmentation models. The four buyer types portrayed here are synthesized from multiple studies and the author's twenty-four years of healthcare experience. The studies and articles that form the basis of the model are: (a) V. K. Rangan, R. T. Moriarty, and G. S. Swartz, "Segmenting Customers in Mature Industrial Markets," *Journal of Marketing* (1992); (b) J. Anderson and J. Narus, *Flexible Market Offerings: Naked Solutions, With Options* (Institute for the Study of Business Markets, Pennsylvania State University, February 18, 1994); (c) T. Verhallen, "Strategy-Based Segmentation of Industrial Markets," *Industrial Marketing Management* 27.4 (1998): 305–13; (d) R. A. Palmer and P. Millier, "Segmentation: Identification, Intuition, and Implementation," *Industrial Marketing Management* 33 (2004): 779–85; and (e) C. Provines, "Understand the 5 Secrets of a Chief Procurement Officer," *The Journal of Professional Pricing*, First Quarter, 2010.

PART IV

SELL AND DEFEND VALUE

Chapter 9

ALIGN WITH THE CUSTOMER BUYING PROCESS

By failing to prepare, you are preparing to fail.

—Benjamin Franklin[1]

At this point, hopefully, you've realized that this book is about a different approach to selling and defending value. We've approached selling and defending value from the customer's perspective. Specifically, we focus on how an organization buys goods and services. As provider supply chains mature, being able to navigate your customer's buying process and the new buyer is going to be increasingly important.

This is not to say that selling to the users will be unimportant. The users of your solution—whether they are physicians or laboratory technicians or hospital IT managers—will always be an important influence in the buying decision. However, the times of selling primarily or only to the user are largely over.

This chapter is about using your understanding of the customer's buying process, the buying center members, the customer's sourcing strategies, and your value to educate the customer. It is about helping them make an informed buying decision. Hopefully, you can be seen as part of the solution, and not just as another salesperson pushing a product or service.

ALIGN VALUE SELLING ACTIVITIES WITH CUSTOMER BUYING STAGE

It's a familiar story. A healthcare supplier believes they offer a superior solution. The solution not only provides clinical benefits but also can save the hospital money. Yet the sales team is unable to communicate the financial benefits because they have not been armed with supporting data.

The company's marketing department decides to invest in economic models or selling tools. The company hires a consultant and spends a lot of money on a selling tool. The tool is rolled out at a national sales meeting, to great fanfare. The training focuses on how to input data into the tool and manipulate assumptions. Six months after rolling out the tool, the company finds that only five percent of the sales team actually uses it.

What went wrong? As the story often goes, there is some finger-pointing. The marketing team says the sales team lacks the skills and knowledge needed to sell in the new market. The sales team says the tool is unrealistic, too complicated, or becomes outdated too quickly. Usually, there is some truth in both perspectives.

Often, however, the bigger issue is that there is no clear direction for how to use the tool and information in the selling process. Sometimes this is because there isn't a clear selling process. Other times this is the result of the selling process being misaligned with the customer buying process.

So, rather than think about this from your own perspective, you should think about it from the customer's perspective. This means considering how the customer makes buying decisions. If your goals are to help the customer improve their business, help them make an informed buying decision, and be seen as an expert resource for them, then you need to understand their buying process.

In chapter 3, we discussed the customer's buying stages and what the customer is trying to achieve at each stage. As a refresher, the buying process usually follows a series of logical stages. It's important to understand what the customer is trying to do at each stage.

Figure 9.1. Align value selling with customer buying process

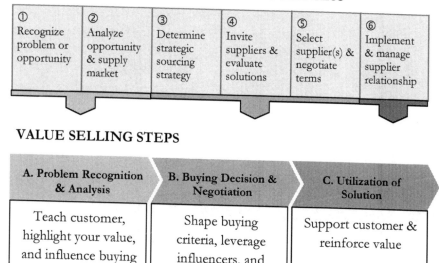

KEY STAGES OF CUSTOMER BUYING PROCESS

① Recognize problem or opportunity	② Analyze opportunity & supply market	③ Determine strategic sourcing strategy	④ Invite suppliers & evaluate solutions	⑤ Select supplier(s) & negotiate terms	⑥ Implement & manage supplier relationship

VALUE SELLING STEPS

A. Problem Recognition & Analysis	B. Buying Decision & Negotiation	C. Utilization of Solution
Teach customer, highlight your value, and influence buying center	Shape buying criteria, leverage influencers, and negotiate	Support customer & reinforce value

At each stage of the customer's buying process, there are different ways to potentially engage the customer to educate them and use your value proposition. This is because at each stage of the buying process, the customer typically has a different "job-to-be-done." In other words, at each stage, the customer is usually trying to complete some buying task so that they can move to the next stage. If you understand the task they are trying to complete, you have a better chance of influencing them.

Over the course of this buying process, the customer's understanding of the problem or opportunity can evolve as they learn more. This is part of the customer education process. It's also your opportunity. However, the customer's evolving understanding of the problem can also be a threat. For example, if your competition is meeting with the customer to educate her about the problem or opportunity, the customer may be led to the competitive solution.

Understanding the customer's buying process should also make you more efficient at selling. For example, if you don't have a relationship with the customer and are asked to participate in a request for proposal (RFP) or tender, you need to ask yourself where the customer is in the buying process. If the customer has reached the stage of sending out an RFP and has done no real evaluation of your solution, you are probably being used in the RFP to reduce the incumbent's price. Alternatively, the customer may be required to obtain a certain number of competitive bids before awarding the contract. In either case, you probably have little chance.

Table 9.1 summarizes the customer's buying stages and how your value proposition can be used at each stage.

Table 9.1. Value Selling Activities at Each Buying Stage

Customer's buying stage and description	Key activities
(1) Recognize problem or opportunity	
Someone in the customer's organization realizes there is a problem or opportunity. The problem or opportunity may not be fully understood.	• Educate the customer on the problem or opportunity • Highlight how other businesses have solved the same problem • Be seen as an expert and resource for the customer • Leverage the buying center and your relationships if you are an incumbent vendor
(2) Analyze opportunity and supply market	
Once the customer recognizes there's a problem or opportunity, they move to the next logical step, which is to qualify the opportunity. They also will try to quantify the financial benefit of solving the problem or capturing the opportunity.	• Highlight your capabilities and expertise • Make the connection to the customer's problem and your differentiated solutions and capability • Continue to help shape the customer's view of the opportunity—quantify the impact of using your solution • Begin to shape the buying criteria

Customer's buying stage and description	Key activities
(3) Determine strategic sourcing strategy	
Based on the supply market, suppliers, and the spend, the customer will determine the sourcing strategy for the supply item. This will include the buying criteria.	• Help shape the buying criteria and sourcing strategy • Provide proof points, evidence or case studies that support the buying criteria
(4) Evaluate suppliers' solutions	
Once there is a list of qualified suppliers, the customer will invite vendors to bid or tender. This may be done through a request for proposal (RFP), request for quotation (RFQ), or tender process. This could be a very formal or informal process depending on the customer.	• Use your value story to differentiate your solution • Tailor your value proposition to the underlying account buying behavior • This is where return on investment or value selling tools may be helpful • If you have no relationship and are invited to bid at this point, question whether you are really a contender • If you are a non-incumbent vendor and believe there is a real chance, consider preparing a change management plan to show the customer you are serious about making them successful
(5) Select supplier and negotiate terms	
Here the customer will go through a process of selecting a supplier, and then negotiating terms with the supplier.	• Use value story, value calculators to reinforce your value • Use your negotiation trades and flexible offers • Highlight the value of the trades
(6) Implement solution and manage supplier relationship	
Finally, the customer will implement the solution and conduct supplier relationship management activities. These include monitoring supplier performance, and supplier development.	• Capture and provide regular updates to the customer on the value that you have delivered • Consider a supplier scorecard to highlight your performance • If you are a non-incumbent, look for opportunities for dissatisfaction with the incumbent supplier

Have a Change Plan

In many situations, the customer may have to make changes in order to realize the value you propose. The change could be a new way of doing business, a new process, or a new vendor. One of the biggest issues for buyers is changing suppliers or doing business differently. This is especially true when converting to a new supplier. The inability to get users to purchase from the new supply agreement is sometimes called purchasing leakage or maverick buying.

One way to bolster the buyer's confidence is to prepare a change management plan. This is simply a plan for how you will work with the customer to achieve the agreed-upon goals. This may include specific training plans, service levels, the number of sales representatives who will support the account, and other service factors. A professional plan will give the buyer confidence and show that you are a serious supplier.

In fact, in some markets and with sophisticated buyers, a change management plan is required in the tender or RFP submission. While this has been the case for large capital purchasing for some time, it is now becoming more common for other types of purchases such as implantable devices. The customer request for a change management plan shows a fair level of sophistication in the buying process. It usually signals that the customer is a serious buyer.

TRIGGERS OF BUYING PROCESS

Customers go through these buying stages in many different ways. For example, the customer's supply-chain staff may attend a conference where they learn about current best practices for sourcing and existing market pricing for spinal implants. Based on these insights, the supply chain director may recognize an opportunity.

Perhaps she recognizes that her hospital has been overpaying for these implants based on what she heard at the conference. This buyer is in the opportunity recognition stage. This opportunity recognition could ultimately lead to a new sourcing initiative and an RFP. If you're the incumbent, this could mean trouble if you are overcharging this customer.

On the other hand, an existing supplier could educate the customer about an opportunity. For instance, a diagnostic manufacturer who has a new blood test that accurately diagnoses ischemic stroke may spend time educating the hospital about the cost and effectiveness of existing diagnostics for stroke. This could include highlighting the impact of poor diagnosis on the customer's value-based purchasing incentives and hospital costs. This wouldn't be a product- or solution-focused presentation, but rather one that leads the customer to recognize that a problem exists.

Purchasing consultants are usually another source of "creating" opportunities. Since they are paid to reduce costs and often share in savings, they have an interest in creating new needs. These consultants often go to senior-level people in the customer organization with the promise of significant cost savings. They are creating the opportunity and educating the customer.

As you can see from these examples, recognition of a problem or opportunity can come from many sources. You can create this recognition. Consultants or competitors can create this recognition. The customer can create this recognition on their own. If the problem or need recognition does not come from you, you can often be put on the defensive. This is because you will end up responding to someone else's agenda. This is a dangerous place to be.

In total, there can be many triggers of a customer beginning a buying process or an evaluation of current purchasing practices. Here are the typical triggers of the process:[2]

- Purchasing consultants
- Peer benchmarking
- Expiring contract
- Competitive selling activity
- Physician request
- Publications or studies
- Conferences
- Benchmarking services
- Group purchasing organization

- Routine strategic sourcing programs
- Cost-saving programs
- Routine value analysis activities
- Quality improvement or lean programs
- Reimbursement cuts

Furthermore, the buying stages aren't always linear. For example, a hospital that is buying surgical gauze may not start at Stage 1. They may simply have a standard sourcing process whereby they send each supply category out to bid every three years. In this case, there is no problem or opportunity recognition. In addition, for surgical gauze there may be many pre-qualified suppliers, and therefore there may be no need to search for or qualify suppliers. Here, the buying process would start in Stage 4.

CUSTOMIZE YOUR MESSAGE

In light of the evolution of the buying process and the emerging role of the economic buyer, it's likely that many different groups or people will join in the buying decision. Therefore, you must customize your message to the needs and interests of the different groups involved. As an example, the buying decision for a new technology that creates an entirely new procedure or service line in the hospital will involve many different stakeholders.

Physicians, a supply chain or purchasing lead, a finance lead, and someone from the service line are likely to be involved in the decision. They may all sit on the value analysis committee or new technology committee. However, they may have different needs and information requirements.

The finance lead may be the CFO, who has a big-picture strategic view and is interested in the growth of important new service lines. The physicians may be interested in innovating with the new technology. The supply chain person may be concerned about the costs of the new technology, the supply continuity, and the inventory management.

Thus it's important to think through the needs and interests of each of these stakeholders and be prepared to customize your message to each. Table 9.2 provides a simple template for thinking through your messaging.

Table 9.2. Example of Message Customization Template

Stakeholder and problem or need	Insights or facts for customer . . .	Questions to lead with . . .
Physicians		
• Be seen as thought leaders • Grow a new service • Attract patients	• New procedure will add 15–25 cases per month • Will only train 100 physicians in first 2 years	• How important is it to attract new patients? • What is the value of each new patient to the practice?
CFO		
• Develop profitable new service lines • Minimize capital investment • Compete against local hospitals	• New procedure has contribution margin of $800 per case • Investment in equipment less than $150,000 • Typical payback period is less than 12 months	• How important is it to attract new patients? • How does the hospital think about the value of each new patient? • How does this procedure compare with others financially?
Supply chain leader		
• Ensure supply continuity • Inventory management of expensive items • Drive cost savings	• Inventory will be on consignment • Supplier will handle all inventory management • Discounts available for volume purchases	• How important is vendor-managed inventory? • How much value does the hospital see in not having to invest in inventory?
Service line leader		
• Impact on hospital quality ratings • Service-line quality perception	• Offer a new treatment alternative for patient population • High procedure-success rates and excellent safety results • Help hospital brand	• How important are new service lines to the hospital's brand and reputation? • What is the impact of a new service offering to the hospital?

The table above provides a simplified example as a starter. It is usually helpful to get a group of people together with a cross-functional view to fully flesh out this template. Also, remember that with all of the changes in healthcare, how customers perceive value may be very different. For some hospitals, attracting patients and building new service lines are important. For other hospitals, the goal is to keep patients out of the hospital. Be sure to understand how the hospital is reimbursed and the hospital's mix of patients.

FOCUS ON OUTCOMES

Theodore Levitt, a marketing scholar, said, "People buy products in order to solve problems. Products are problem solving tools." In his book *The Marketing Imagination,* Levitt cites the famous quote "the customer buys a quarter inch hole not a quarter inch drill bit."[3] In a similar way, Charles Revson of Revlon, Inc., said, "In the factory we make cosmetics. In the store we sell hope."[4] Both examples illustrate that the customer is buying something other than a physical product.

In the case of the drill bit, the hole is the outcome the customer is buying. The customer is not buying a drill bit. You should apply this same thinking to your solution and how you communicate this to the customer. Whether you sell an implantable device, tongue depressors, or a hospital information system, the customer is seeking a certain outcome.

The customer has a job-to-get-done and an outcome to achieve. Your communications and language should be consistent with the outcome the customer is trying to achieve. The outcomes can be clinical, economic, emotional, or a combination of these.

There's another important point about outcomes. You should frame what it takes to achieve an outcome, and use this frame to differentiate your company and solution. Typically, an outcome is a function of four factors: people, process, technology, and education. In other words, to get a successful outcome you need more than just a product. You need a combination of these four drivers. These are illustrated in Figure 9.2.

Figure 9.2. Four drivers of cost and quality outcomes

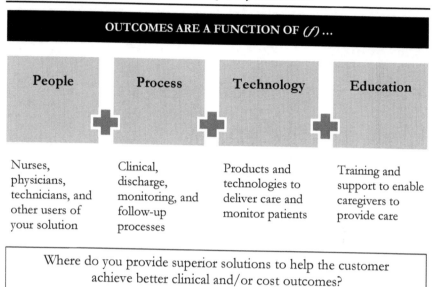

OUTCOMES ARE A FUNCTION OF (f) **...**			
People	**Process**	**Technology**	**Education**
Nurses, physicians, technicians, and other users of your solution	Clinical, discharge, monitoring, and follow-up processes	Products and technologies to deliver care and monitor patients	Training and support to enable caregivers to provide care

> Where do you provide superior solutions to help the customer achieve better clinical and/or cost outcomes?

In order to understand this, think about a successful clinical outcome for an open-heart surgery. First, you need people—nurses, physicians, and other healthcare professionals. Process is next. Good process matters. The hospital needs the right process for pre-op, the operation, and post-op to achieve the best outcomes. Next comes the technology. There's a lot of technology that goes into getting a good outcome. Finally, there's education—the training of staff and caregivers involved before, during, and after the surgery.

It takes a combination of these factors to achieve an outcome. Focusing on outcomes from the customer's perspective may open your eyes to new areas where you have advantages. Using this simple framing that outcomes are a function of people, process, technology, and education may help you to frame your value.

For example, a company that sells a surgical instrument or orthopaedic implant may offer little differentiation in the device itself. However, the company may have a vastly superior sales force and customer training. It could be these areas of sales support and training that provide the real differentiation. So, in this case, the company could frame its differentiation in terms of how their training and support are key drivers of successful outcomes.

USE YOUR CAPABILITIES AND OTHER LEVERS

There are some nuances to engaging the customer and using levers to influence the customer's buying decision. Some of these nuances involve leveraging your unique capabilities. Capabilities are simply your company's unique, non-product-specific differentiated strengths. These are things beyond the product or service that you sell—such as your service response time, your supply chain capability, or your innovation pipeline.

Other levers involve using the science behind influence and buyer decision-making. These include the principles of blemishes, loss aversion, decision framing, and scarcity. I briefly introduce these well-studied principles and discuss how to use them during the buying process.

Examples of Supply Chain Capability

A large hospital system wanted to standardize on equipment used across the system.[5] During the evaluation stage of the buying process, one particular supplier of equipment was the clear front-runner. This supplier had a technological advantage, which the customer really liked. Since this customer was one of the top hospital systems in the US, this potential deal likely meant a sizable amount of business for the supplier.

As part of the evaluation process, the hospital system wanted to evaluate the supplier's supply chain. The customer went to visit the factory where the equipment was manufactured. This is not an uncommon practice in many industries. Suppliers often offer or allow customers to visit manufacturing or R&D facilities to help educate them about the supplier's capabilities. It usually is meant to be a way to sell the total value of a relationship with the supplier.

In this example, the hospital VP of Supply Chain visited the manufacturing facility. The VP happened to be very tenured and experienced, with deep expertise. He had a broad set of experiences in supply chain beyond the hospital industry. This included experience in other industries where it is important to understand potential suppliers' supply chain strategy, capabilities, and sources of supply.

During the manufacturing site visit, the hospital VP of Supply Chain was shown the manufacturing line for the equipment his hospital system preferred. Remember that his hospital system really liked one particular technological advantage that this supplier offered that others did not. The technological advantage turned out to be driven by one simple component of the equipment.

During the tour of the manufacturing process, the hospital VP of Supply Chain asked a simple question: "Who is your supplier for that part?" The tour guide told him that they only had one supplier, who had taken a long time to qualify.

While this was an honest answer, it didn't sell the value of the supplier. The savvy VP immediately recognized that he would be at significant risk if he standardized on this particular equipment. What if the small company supplying this critical component to the equipment manufacturer couldn't, for some reason?

Supply disruption happens all the time, whether because of accidents, natural disasters, or other factors. If you live on the east coast of the US or know someone who does, remember what happened during Hurricane Sandy in 2012. Supply disruptions occurred in many areas of the economy.

In this case, the equipment manufacturer had no alternative suppliers for this critical component. If a supply disruption with this small supplier occurred, the equipment manufacturer might be unable to supply the hospital system. Patient care could be put at risk.

Although the hospital system preferred this supplier's equipment, it couldn't move forward with the supplier. The hospital system needed assurances that the supplier could find and qualify alternative sources of supply for the critical component.

In the end, the manufacturer found and qualified alternative sources of supply for the critical component. This allowed the hospital system to move forward with this supplier. This story highlights the importance of capabilities as a selling point and as risk.

Perhaps your product itself is not clearly differentiated, but your supply chain capability is the source of differentiation. In this story, the product was differentiated, but the supply chain was a risk. It took a savvy supply-chain executive from the customer to see the risks in the supplier's manufacturing strategy.

Let's consider the opposite case. A larger supplier of medical supplies with a significant market position was in the midst of negotiations with a large group purchasing organization (GPO) in the US. As was typical at the time, the GPO was threatening to give a sole source position to a smaller supplier if the large company did not lower its price. During the preparation for the bid and during the negotiations, much of the large supplier's focus was on the product-to-product value comparison. The large supplier believed that it had a better product in some areas, but in many areas the products were relatively similar.

This product-to-product comparison generated much internal pressure to lower the price in order to avoid losing the business. It wasn't until someone asked a simple question—"Can the small supplier actually supply the market if they were awarded the contract?"—that the large company started to understand its position.

After analysis, the large company realized that the small supplier lacked the infrastructure, resources, and manufacturing capability to actually supply the market. The GPO threat was a simple negotiation tactic. Now the large supplier had a different framing of its value proposition. The value was not just the product advantages that it had; it included the ability to continuously supply the market.

Other Capability Examples

Beyond supply chain, there are other capabilities you should consider as levers. Take innovation as an example. A medical device company with a more robust pipeline of solutions than its competitors may have a distinct advantage. The supplier may have to prioritize customers when it launches a new technology because of constraints on manufacturing capacity or physician training.

This supplier could use its pipeline capability as a lever. It may not be possible to offer all customers access to new technologies at the same time. It would be natural for the supplier to want to provide priority access to those customers with whom it has a good relationship. So, in this case, the innovation capability could be a lever.

One simple exercise you should try for your company is to list all of those capabilities where you have a distinct advantage. Broadly speaking, capabilities can fall into these categories:

- Supply chain
- Innovation
- Services
- Training and education
- Technical support

It's important to consider differences in capabilities from the customer's perspective. The number of alternative suppliers and the type of supply you sell will play a role in how important these capabilities are to the customer.

Shape Purchasing Criteria

Be honest about differences between your and your competitors' solutions and capabilities as well as the importance of these to the customer. If you believe there are important differences, then you need to educate the customer about them. Ideally, you should get this information into the buying criteria.

Somewhere between buying stages 1 and 4, the customer is determining the criteria for the buying decision. These can be very formal, and driven by the customer's policy or laws. For example, in the European Union, there are rules that govern how public tenders should operate. On the other hand, buying criteria or rules may be relatively informal. However, in the case of a real competitive bid, the customer will almost always base the buying decision on some criteria. Figure 9.3 is an example for a CT scanner replacement:[6]

Figure 9.3. Example of RFP/tender scorecard

Project:	CT Scanner Replacement		Review date:	20-Jan	
Sourcing Team Lead:			Bid Round:	Second	
Category	**Weight**	**Evaluation items**	**Vendor 1**	**Vendor 2**	**Vendor 3**
Quality	30%	Image quality			
		Dose			
		Technical performance			
		Point Score (100 = highest)	91	62	78
Price / Costs	35%	Acquisition price			
		Service costs			
		Parts & repair			
		Trade-in value			
		Point Score (100 = highest)	50	80	90
Warranty & Support	20%	Warranty			
		Service quality			
		Guaranteed response time			
		Training			
		Point Score (100 = highest)	83	60	70
Project Team	15%	Experience			
		References			
		Point Score (100 = highest)	80	50	75
Total Score			73.4	66.1	80.2

If you can't influence the formal buying criteria, you've missed a big opportunity. In some formal purchasing processes, such as tender markets in certain countries, the customer must follow established tender criteria or an established process. It's not uncommon in some situations to see criteria established for which only one supplier really qualifies. This is because the supplier shaped the criteria.

If you do have a real advantage in technology or capabilities, then you need to work with the customer well in advance of the development of the buying criteria. In some cases, this might be 12 to 18 months in advance of the issue of the RFP or tender. If you have a unique technology, you could try to convince the customer to carve the technology out of the RFP or tender. This way you are really competing against yourself.

One supplier had a real advantage in training surgeons. They regularly offered training for new and existing surgeons at key accounts. When the tender criteria were put together for a key account, guess what happened? Training ended up as a key factor in the tender with a very high weighting. Since this company had a real advantage in training, they were able to leverage this strength in the tender process.

Develop and Use Good Questions

If you have a good value story and a tool to support it, it may be tempting to lead with the tool. There are a couple of problems with this. First, you'll be talking at the customer rather than listening to them. Second, many tools focus on what the seller is selling rather than on the problem the customer is trying to solve.

More important, the problem or opportunity may be one that the customer doesn't even know exists. Put yourself in the customer's shoes. If a supplier showed up with a selling tool that was focused on their solution, it would look like they were trying to push a solution rather than solve a problem. You first must get the customer to recognize the problem or opportunity. After that, the discussion should be about how you can solve it better than anyone else.

Peter Drucker, the business expert, said, "My greatest strength as a consultant is to be ignorant and ask a few questions."[7] Asking good questions can be a tool to better understand the customer's problem or opportunity as well as to lead the customer where you want to go. For your business, it might help to develop a good set of questions and align them with the customer buying process.

Ideally, this is best done with an understanding of the customer's operations and business situation. In addition, you should be leading them to where your advantages lie. As an example, let's use the supplier who had the supply chain advantage that we just discussed. Rather than walk in and tell the customer how important supply chain reliability is to them, you might ask questions to help uncover how important it is for them:

- How important is continuous supply to your hospital?

- If you had a supply disruption, what would happen?

- How would supply disruption impact patient care, your business, and the hospital's image?

- How do you currently evaluate supply chain capability for your suppliers?

This is a simplified example, but hopefully you get the point. Asking good questions should help uncover opportunities and lead the customer where you want them to go. In this example, asking these types of questions may prompt the customer to think about adding supply chain capability criteria to the buying process.

A tenured salesperson told about selling a solution to a senior executive at a hospital. The salesperson set up a meeting with the senior executive. The executive was obviously very busy, and was double-booked. He told the salesperson, "You have thirty seconds—tell me what you want." The salesperson replied, "Will you give me one minute if I can tell you how to cut your emergency room waiting time in half?" The hospital executive responded, "I'd give you a half-day if you can help me do that!"

Be Honest; Sometimes a Negative Is a Positive

Being honest and presenting a balanced view of your product or solution is critical. Most solutions create both positive and negative value for customers. Sometimes it's tempting to omit the negative value items and present a "powerful" value story of only the positive elements. This can raise a red flag with buyers and make them skeptical. In addition, in many companies, legal and regulatory departments will force the presentation of a balanced view.

However, there is another reason to be honest about your flaws. In experiments in consumer buying behavior, marketing researchers discovered that presenting some negative information actually improves the likelihood of purchase.

In their experiment, the researchers used a consumer good—hiking boots. One group of consumers received only positive information about the boots: their durability, orthopaedic soles, waterproof materials, and so forth. The other group received the same positive information, but also some negative information—the limited number of colors available.

Those in the group that received only positive information were less likely to purchase than those in the group that received both positive and negative information.[8]

It appeared in the experiment that the negative information helped highlight or accentuate the positive information. Obviously, the negative information should be minor in comparison to the positive information. Likewise, the negatives should be non-core to the value story. The negatives should also be presented at the end, after the positive information.

Being honest enhances the believability of your value story. The boot story was a consumer experiment. But any professional buyer who has seen a vendor return on investment or value tool will tell you that a completely one-sided presentation makes them suspicious. They then have to dig and look for areas where your solution is not so good. It will also make them wonder what else you might not be forthcoming about.

Loss Aversion, Decision Framing, and Scarcity

While it would be nice to assume that we are all completely rational in our decision making, in real life this turns out not to be the case. People make seemingly irrational decisions all the time. Understanding what drives such behavior may help you sell and defend your value.

The first dynamic to understand is loss aversion. The basic idea is that people value avoiding losses much more than they value achieving gains.[9] The framing of the decision and reference point becomes very important. For example, if you were launching a new medical device that reduced in-hospital costs, you could frame its value in different ways to the hospital:

- You will save five hundred dollars per patient by using this device.
- You are losing five hundred dollars per patient by not using this new device.

The first statement is framed as a gain. It implies that by taking action, the buyer will see some savings in the future. The second statement is framed as the stopping of a loss. It draws attention to the financial losses already occurring. It makes the buyer think, how am I losing five hundred dollars per patient?

In countless studies of consumers, researchers show that consumers prefer avoiding losses much more than achieving gains. Some studies suggest that loss aversion may be tied to experience and may diminish over time.[10] Other studies show that loss aversion may diminish when one is deciding for others.[11] Remember the saying "no one ever got fired for buying IBM?" Buying IBM was considered a job-loss-avoidance strategy.

As another example, consider how a medical technology company with a new-to-the-world technology might frame its value. Let's say that this new technology allowed hospitals to create a new service line. One framing to the hospital could be the number of new patients the service line may attract. You could certainly estimate the direct impact of the new procedure as well as the value of attracting new patients. These new patients would likely have follow-up visits that generate revenue. The other approach would be to frame the potential loss in patients and revenue if the competing hospital down the street had the new service line but this hospital did not. This would be framing the new technology as a possible loss. The hospital down the street could draw patients away.

Another dynamic to consider is scarcity. In the US, before Christmas each year, we see the rule of scarcity play out. Seemingly normal people trample and fight each other to get the special deal on the newest electronic item or hot new toy. In this case, there is a time pressure along with scarcity. The store has only so many of the hot toys available on the designated day.

In the consumer world, scarcity of an item or service generally makes it more valuable, and people are willing to pay more for it. According to Robert Cialdini in his book *Influence*, there are two reasons for this. The availability of an item or service can signal its quality. The less there is of it, the more valuable it must be. Second, as things become scarce, we lose freedom. We respond by wanting to have it more.[12]

Think about your product portfolio, innovation pipeline, and range of services. If all of these are offered to every customer, you've created no scarcity. Certain services may be highly valuable and differentiated. If you create the perception of scarcity, this may cause buyers to want them more. In real life, companies that launch new technologies may be forced to create scarcity because of regulatory constraints, manufacturing capacity, or training constraints. You should use this scarcity to your advantage.

An in-depth discussion of these topics is beyond the scope of this book. You should, however, recognize that these dynamics might be in play and use them to your advantage. Consider developing alternative messaging and testing it with different customers.

PUT YOUR MONEY WHERE YOUR MOUTH IS

Customers are tired of hearing how great your solution is or how much money they're going to save by using it. Many vendors make these claims. As a hospital executive said, "I'm very skeptical. We've been burned too many times by expensive technologies that don't work or have real outcomes that are different than what was promised."[13] One way to prove that you believe in your value is to provide some kind of assurance. This could be a guarantee, a risk-reward arrangement, an agreement to performance penalties, or other some form of having some skin in the game. It is common practice for suppliers in other industries to provide monetary assurances. In general, the following are types of value assurances.

Outcomes risk sharing. In this case, the supplier has a risk contract tied to the customer achieving an outcome. In healthcare, the outcome could be a patient outcome, cost savings, or a process outcome. For example, a diagnostics testing company selling high-cost genomic tests provided insurers a guarantee of the proportion of patients who would receive chemotherapy based on the diagnostic test result. If the percentage of patients receiving chemotherapy exceeded a certain threshold, the testing company would lower the pre-negotiated price for the test.[14] In this case, this could be considered a process guarantee. The company was agreeing that the proportion of patients following a certain care pathway directed by the test results would not exceed a certain threshold. They did not guarantee specific patient outcomes.

Performance guarantees. Many products or solutions play a critical role in the diagnosis and treatment of patients. For some capital equipment areas such as imaging and laboratory, the uptime performance of the equipment is critical to the hospital's efficiency. Any equipment downtime causes lost productivity, higher costs, and risks to patient care. In some cases, customers look to suppliers for specific guarantees related to equipment uptime. Any performance below a certain threshold results in a penalty. In other situations, customers recognize that suppliers' ability to provide a continuous supply of product is critical to their operation. Any supply disruption could be expensive in terms of finding alternative sources of supply and managing these vendors. Savvy customers have started to ask for specific supply-chain performance guarantees for supply continuity. For example, the customer will build a penalty into the contract if the supplier is unable to supply a particular item.

Any decision to enter into risk-sharing or performance guarantees should be well thought out. Outcomes-related risk arrangements often require both the supplier and the customer to take specific actions in order to achieve the outcome. These arrangements are generally costly and time-consuming for both the customer and supplier. Therefore, they shouldn't be entered into without careful consideration.

Performance guarantees could allow a supplier to leverage its strengths. For example, if you were a supplier of capital equipment and your mean time between failure (MTBF) was vastly superior to your competitor's, it would be much easier and less costly for you to provide a guarantee of equipment uptime. Your competitor with an inferior solution may have many more failures that require a significant investment in service costs. You could leverage your strength by assuring the uptime value.

KEY TAKEAWAYS

- It's important to align your value selling with the customer's buying process.

- Early in the buying process, the customer is discovering a problem or an opportunity. This is your chance to educate the customer and lead them to your solution.

- Your value proposition is not just the differentiated value your product or solution provides. It also includes your unique, differentiated capabilities as a firm.

- Developing questions that allow you to uncover customer problems and lead them to your solution is important. This is particularly true early in the buying process.

- It's important to be honest about the value you provide to customers. This includes both positive and negative elements of value.

- Suppliers need to think through whether it makes sense to guarantee value as well as how to customize their message to different stakeholders.

NOTES

1. www.brainyquote.com (accessed February 7, 2014).

2. Adapted from "The Benefits of a Successful Value Analysis Program" [Webcast], *WellStar*, www.iienet.org (accessed November 2, 2013).

3. T. Levitt, *The Marketing Imagination* (exp. ed.) (Free Press, 1986).

4. Ibid.

5. D. Hargraves, "Making a Good Supplier Better through Sustainable Supplier Development," presentation at Next Level Purchasing Conference, September 2013.

6. Adapted from C. Dominick and S. Lunney, *The Procurement Game Plan* (J. Ross Publishing, 2012); and CT Scanner RFP Kona Community Hospital, www.kch.hhsc.org (accessed December 20, 2013).

7. Rick Wartzman, "How to Consult Like Peter Drucker," *Forbes.com*, September 11, 2012 (accessed November 2, 2013).

8. Cited in B. Snyder, "The Positive Effects of Negative Information" [Blog], Stanford Graduate School of Business, June 1, 2011, www.gsb.stanford.edu (accessed November 2, 2013).

9. A. Tversky and D. Kahneman, "Advances in Prospect Theory: Cumulative Representation of Uncertainty," *Journal of Risk and Uncertainty* 5 (1992): 297–323.

10. J. A. List, "Does Market Experience Eliminate Market Anomalies?," *Quarterly Journal of Economics* 118 (2003): 41–71.

11. E. Polman, "Self–Other Decision Making and Loss Aversion," *Organizational Behavior and Human Decision Processes* 119.2 (2012): 141–50.

12. R. B. Cialdini, *Influence: Science and Practice* (Boston, MA: Pearson Education, 2008).

13. C. Provines, "Smart Purchasing: Evolving Hospital Buying and Implications for Suppliers" (Working paper, 2014).

14. J. Carlson, L. Garrison, and S. Sullivan, "Paying for Outcomes: Innovative Coverage and Reimbursement Schemes for Pharmaceuticals," *Journal of Managed Care Pharmacy*, October 2009.

Chapter | 10

RECOGNIZE AND LEARN TO PLAY BUYER GAMES

Defense is a definite part of the game, and a great part of defense is learning to play it without fouling.

—John Wooden[1]

As professional buyers play a greater role in the buying decision and process, the likelihood that you will encounter buying games increases. This is because professional buyers have found it relatively easy to use games and sourcing tactics to extract value from unsuspecting suppliers. Sometimes it's so easy, there's no need for buyers to do any of the hard work of real strategic sourcing.

For example, have you ever been the incumbent vendor in a request for proposal (RFP) process and had the sneaking suspicion that the RFP is a sham? Maybe it was a rushed RFP. Alternatively, it could have been an RFP that the users knew nothing about. In fact, using RFPs as leverage to reduce the incumbent vendor's price is one of the simplest tricks used by professional buyers.

A purchasing manager highlighted this as one of his key tactics. He said that he selects the supplier he wants to use in advance. It is usually a high-value, high-priced supplier. He then adds many other suppliers into the RFP process. His hope is that he receives a low bid from one of these other suppliers. He then uses the low bid as leverage to reduce his preferred supplier's price.[2]

This chapter is meant to provide you with insights into the games, tricks, and tactics you are likely to see. Some suggested counter-moves and ideas are provided as well. Although the chapter captures a fair number of common games, there are other games, tricks, and variations out there.

Much of what we have discussed so far is meant to be a foundation for defending your value against buyer tricks and games. Understanding your value, defining trades, and preparing an offering strategy are all critical. In addition, understanding the buying center, the buying process, and the influence of different people involved in the buying decision should give you the confidence to successfully play games with buyers.

TWELVE BASIC BUYER GAMES, AND HOW TO PLAY

There are literally dozens of tricks and tactics buyers can use. So, as a supplier, how do you begin to recognize these? And once you're able to recognize the games, how do you play them?

There are three general categories of games and tactics to consider. First are strategic sourcing tactics. These include tactics like RFPs and reverse auctions. Next are tactics intended to manipulate perceptions. These include intentional delays and questioning your value. Finally, there are tough tactics. These include canceling agreements and playing good cop / bad cop.

Table 10.1 details twelve common buyers games and tactics.[3]

Table 10.1. Twelve Common Buyer Games and Counter-Moves

Tactic, details, and goals . . .	How you could respond . . .
Question your value or complain about quality or service	
• Whether real or a bluff, question your value or quality	• If the buyer is fishing, don't give up information
• They will fish for information to use against you	• Be honest and open if you've had real issues with this customer
• Any information you provide can be used as leverage against you	• Don't argue; ask questions to understand
	• Return to your value proposition
Delay	
• Intentionally delay the buying process	• Don't offer additional discounts to close the deal—this teaches the buyer to slow down even more
• Slow things down in the hopes that you will offer incentives to move things along	• Never disclose your current sales performance
	• Probe for reasons for delay; be patient
Deadlines	
• The buyer sets a deadline for your "best and final offer"	• Look at their past history: do they continue to negotiate past the "best and final" deadline, or is that it?
• The buyer's goal is often to cut short the back-and-forth negotiations	• Watch for buyers who say they want your best and final offer and then continue to negotiate from there
Cooling-off period	
• Buyer formally announces a cooling-off period in the negotiations or buying as a way to pressure the seller	• Try to understand the reasons behind the cooling-off period—is it real, or is it a simple negotiation tactic?
• Sellers hate to be out of touch, and fear the worst	• Remember, professional buyers are often under pressure to get contracts signed as well
• The buyer hopes this speeds up the concession process	

Tactic, details, and goals . . .	How you could respond . . .
False RFPs when you are the incumbent	
• Issue RFP to multiple suppliers with no real intention of switching • They hope to obtain a low bid to use as leverage against you	• Ask about their policies; they could be required to issue RFPs above a certain spend level • Understand your value differences and switching costs • Be prepared to trade value or use multiple offers of differing value
False RFPs when you are on the outside	
• Request that you participate in the RFP process when you've had little or no history with the account • They hope to use a low price from you to lower the incumbent's price	• Ask about their policies; they could be required to issue RFPs above a certain spend level • Request meetings with all of the key members of the buying center as well as product evaluations • If they won't give you access, this is a sign that they are not serious about you as a supplier
Budget reduction	
• Buyer says that their budget was just reduced and they need suppliers to sharpen their pencils	• Offer to lower price by changing the offering or using your trades
Intimidation techniques	
• The buyer uses good cop / bad cop, dark rooms, bright lights, low chair, or other techniques to put you on the defensive	• Call out the behavior—"it feels like . . ." • Change the setting or take a time-out • Ask for more comfortable surroundings

Tactic, details, and goals . . .	How you could respond . . .
Price caps	
• The buyer specifies the most that they are willing to pay for an item or service	• Get clear on specifications—make sure that it is an apples-to-apples comparison
• This tactic is usually reserved for situations where it's hard for the buyer to get users to standardize on one or two suppliers	• Shape the specifications in advance if possible
• Their goal is to get at least one vendor to agree to sell at that price and use this as leverage	• Unbundle and take things of value out of the proposal if possible
Reverse auction	
• Buyer sets up an electronic auction where sellers bid for the business	• Decide whether it makes sense to participate
• Their goal is to use low auction bids to force down all prices	• Remember that reverse auctions are usually a sourcing tool for real commodities
• This is usually reserved for commodity items or ones with low switching costs	• Influence the specifications prior to the auction if possible
	• Submit multiple offers—lower value and higher value
Should cost-modeling	
• Buyer reverse-engineers the supplier's cost structure	• Move the conversation to value
• The buyer uses this cost model to determine how much they are willing to pay	• Highlight your value differences
• Their goal is to move to a cost plus a small margin as opposed to a value discussion	• Probe for their real interest—if they need to lower costs, change the offering

Tactic, details, and goals . . .	How you could respond . . .
Consultants	
• Buyer uses third-party consultant to run sourcing event • Their goal is to save money—the third party often gets to share in savings	• Understand who brought the consultant in—procurement, senior management, or some other member of the buying center • Realize that the consultant will use any bid you make with other customers • Unbundle or use multiple offers with differing value and price • Educate or discredit the consultant

SIGNS OF BUYER GAMES

There are many buyer games. Table 10.1 provides an overview of some of the more popular ones. Beyond specific buyer games, you should be looking for the general signs of a bluff. There are a couple of important points to consider for all of the games and tactics. First, in real life, switching suppliers can be a lot of work. It can also be risky—not only for the customer but also for the professional buyer, who faces personal risk if they push to switch suppliers and something goes wrong.

Also, in many cases, the promise of a low price from an outside supplier requires that the customer actually transition their purchases to that low-cost supplier. The inability to move purchasing to the lower-cost supplier is called "leakage," or off-contract buying, or maverick spending. It's a big problem for professional buyers. Studies show that it is one of the reasons strategic sourcing efforts fail.[4]

Another key point is that switching suppliers usually is not done in haste. It typically requires a thoughtful evaluation that can take weeks or months depending on the supply item. It also often requires alignment with all the key members of the buying center. This is why understanding the buying center is so critical.

What are the general signs of purchasing games? You should be looking for these as signs of a potential bluff:

- *Rushed RFP process.* A thorough evaluation of suppliers' solutions takes time and planning. If you're dealing with a rushed RFP, stop and ask whether this is real. Is there a good explanation for the rush? Is there enough time to properly evaluate the solutions?

- *Strange timing for bid response.* As an example, the buyer sends out an RFP two days before Christmas and the response is due the first business day following the holiday. If you were serious about making a purchasing decision, would you do this?

- *No formal evaluation.* The buyer issues an RFP, but no evaluation of the different suppliers' solutions is planned. If you are on the outside, and the buyer really wants you to bid, you need to ask for an evaluation. If they won't evaluate your solution, how serious are they about using you as a supplier?

- *Users not involved.* In this case, the users of the solution are not involved or don't know about the sourcing initiative. This is a sure sign that the buyer is playing games with you. It's hard to switch suppliers and get users to start to use a new supplier, even for simple supply items.

- *Sloppy RFP.* The RFP may be poorly written, contain typos, or use language irrelevant to what the buyer is sourcing. In a training session, one salesperson told a story of an RFP where the buyer changed the name of the RFP but forgot to change the specifications and terms. The RFP details referred to a completely different supply area. It is possible that the buyer was simply sloppy. On the other hand, they may have copied and pasted from another RFP just to get this RFP out.

Understanding the buying dynamic is a critical step in getting paid fairly for the value you bring to your customer. It will also help you improve your sales effectiveness. If you've found yourself responding to RFPs where you have no real chance, think about how you could use that time more effectively. Whether it's spending time with family or growing business with real prospects, the time wasted playing buyer games can certainly be better used.

BEWARE OF SELF-DESTRUCTIVE PRICING

Sometimes you may be a non-preferred supplier and be asked to bid where you know you have no chance. You know the customer has no intention of switching from its preferred supplier. You are simply a pawn in the bidding game. What do you do?

Occasionally, this question is asked to groups of salespeople. Inevitably, someone says, "I submit a really low bid to screw my competitor." Of course this person knows that the buyer will take his low price and use it as leverage against his competitor.

If you were the incumbent supplier in this situation and you found out about the really low bid, what would you think? You'd probably think your competitor is out of control. If you were the incumbent in this situation and had a chance to bid on your competitor's business, you'd be tempted to use a low bid as well.

By playing the game of kamikaze pricing on business you know you don't have a chance of winning, you are hurting yourself. You are also training professional buyers to use this tactic. Finally, remember that purchasing people change jobs, they talk to each other, and they benchmark pricing through many sources. Once you throw that low price out there, it could create a lot of issues for you with customers you want to keep.

PROVIDE OPTIONS

As discussed, smart purchasers understand that suppliers don't just provide a product or service; they provide capabilities. Capabilities are the resources, future innovations, ideas, services, and special ways that a supplier can help the customer meet its goals and succeed.

This is not just a product; it can include supply chain services, innovation, and other services. As a supplier, you don't have an unlimited amount of capabilities at your disposal to provide to every customer. You must decide which customers get which capabilities.

Be upfront and honest about this with customers. This is particularly necessary when you are dealing with professional buyers. On the other side of the table, the professional buyers use a process called supplier relationship management (SRM). They are doing exactly the same thing. They are making choices about which suppliers are strategic and how to build a long-term relationship with them.

So, during the sales and negotiation process, you should be prepared to "name the relationship." This shouldn't be a threat. Rather, it's simply being clear about what a valued relationship with you as a supplier brings. For example, if it's clear that the customer only cares about price (or at least is acting like a price buyer), should you give them priority access to new technologies, or give them special supply-chain services or delivery?

If they truly only care about price or are acting as if they only care about price, you should provide them with an offering that makes sense. Equally important, you should call out what type of relationship the customer is asking for. In other words, be explicit about the type of relationship they are driving towards with their negotiation tactics and ask them if this is what they want.

Figure 10.1. Align offering with the relationship

	Transactional Relationship	Partnership
Products		
• Access to existing product portfolio	Standard	Standard
• Priority access to new technologies	Not Available (N/A)	Standard
Services		
• Basic service & support	Standard	Standard
• 24×7 service	N/A	Optional
• Remote monitoring	N/A	Optional
• Advanced education	N/A	Optional
Partnership Programs		
• Inventory management	N/A	Standard
• Lean process expert support	N/A	Standard
• Customer service specialist	N/A	Standard
• Innovation days	N/A	Standard

Rather than do this on the fly, prepare in advance. A simple example of two types of relationships is illustrated in Figure 10.1. You'll notice that the transactional relationship has nothing included. The goal is to create a stripped-down offering that has no extras. Obviously, you should look for leverage points with the services that you include on the list. For example, if your company doesn't launch many new technologies or doesn't have any in the pipeline, new technologies are not a leverage point.

If you are unsure of the type of relationship the customer wants or if you believe the professional buyer is playing games, consider using multiple offers. This tactic can also be helpful when there is a conflict in the buying center. Perhaps the user wants a different offering than the direction you are receiving from the purchasing agent. In this case, the use of multiple offers forces the conversation.

Be clear about what the relationship is and what comes with it. If something like this does not exist for your company, you can easily create one. Gather a cross-functional team of people together. They should include people from sales, corporate accounts, reimbursement, supply chain, customer education, and marketing. Brainstorm the types of relationships you have with your customers. The two listed in Figure 10.1 are starters. You may have others. Under each relationship column, list the services or offerings to be included. If you've already analyzed your offerings or created negotiation "trades," these should already be defined.

SWITCHING COSTS AND CONSEQUENCES

Switching Costs

Switching costs are the costs and risks a customer incurs when changing from one supplier or supply item to another. It's important to understand and manage the customer's switching costs. This is particularly true when you're the incumbent supplier.

Customers face many cost pressures. The attraction of gaining some price savings by moving from one supplier to another can be powerful. Therefore, it's important to have a handle on the switching costs. This is especially true if you are the incumbent supplier and they are threatening to switch business from you. Switching costs can occur in a number of areas:[5]

- *Sourcing and vendor management costs.* These include administrative costs of setting up new vendors or supply items in the customer's purchasing systems, and managing vendors. These can also include the actual cost of running the sourcing initiative. As an example, it is estimated that going through a full sourcing initiative costs a hospital over $3,000 per contract.[6]

- *Inventory management.* Inventory-related costs for switching suppliers including receiving, storing, counting, moving, and disposing of supply items.

- *Purchasing leaks or maverick buying.* Often the savings promised by switching to a low-priced supplier never materialize because the customer is unable to get the users to purchase from the lower priced supplier. In the purchasing world, these are called leaks, off-contract buying, or maverick buying.

- *Training.* New solutions often require that users and others in the account be trained on a new technology or way of doing something. This can be a significant source of non-value-added or unproductive work.

- *Lost productivity.* Beyond the costs of training users, there is often lower productivity when a new method or process is introduced. This lost productivity is usually not considered when switching from one supplier to another.

- *Bundled price.* The customer may be receiving special pricing across a variety of product categories that is part of a bundled deal or broader relationship. If you are the incumbent supplier and the customer is going to move all or part of your business, you should consider increasing pricing on the remaining items.

- *Access to new technology.* For supply categories where the technology changes rapidly or where there are new technologies on the horizon, buyers need access to these technologies. If the buyer decides to switch from you, you should consider creating consequences.

- *Access to special services.* You should spend some time brainstorming all of the various services, training programs, and other ways you support the customer. Many of these may be of real value to influencers in the account. If the professional buyer is threatening you, these need to be put forth as potential items to be pulled.

- *Risks.* These are sometimes hard to quantify. However, risk is real. Supply disruptions, quality problems, and spotty service levels can disrupt the customer's business and cost them real money.

From an execution standpoint, switching costs can be a powerful tool to use in selling and negotiating value. The point is not to use switching costs as a threat. Rather, it is to make sure that the customer is making a fully informed decision. Therefore, where possible, you should try to estimate the financial impact to the customer of switching.

Table 10.2. Switching Costs

Cost/risk item	Potential customer business impact	Value (quantify)
Train all users on a new system if they switch suppliers	• The hospital has 2,000 users • It takes 30 minutes to train each user • 30 minutes × 2,000 users means 1,000 hours spent training	• Users are paid $40 per hour • Therefore, the cost of training is $40 x 1,000 hours = $40,000

Also, you should look at switching costs carefully. Obviously, you want to frame them differently if you are the incumbent rather than the outsider at an account. Some of the more sophisticated buyers, especially in parts of Europe, now ask sellers to provide a change management plan. This is simply a plan for how the supplier will manage implementation of the new agreement. It is especially important for suppliers who are new or are taking over a much larger portion of the business. Table 10.2 is an example of a format you can use to brainstorm switching costs.

Moreover, managing switching costs is also about creating consequences for the customer's actions. For example, if you are the incumbent vendor with the majority of market share and the customer tells you they are moving most of the business to another supplier, are you still going to provide the same service, price, and support? If you make no changes, you have just helped to lower the customer's switching costs.

Create Consequences—Use Your Trades

When playing buyer games, it's important to have already identified and prioritized your trades. In chapter 7, we discussed creating offers and trades. At this point, you should have a list of trades to use with customers. It's helpful to put the list in a priority order. This way, when the buyer is pushing you for a lower price or asks for something else of value, you can find some way to counter that request or ask for something in exchange.

Trading sends a few signals to the buyer. First, it says that you have some understanding of your value. Second, it says that you are flexible and willing to collaborate to reach an agreement. Last, trading shows that you negotiate with sophistication. Most buyers will respect and see trading as a good thing. Professional buyers who are used to bullying suppliers, on the other hand, may not appreciate your trading.

There is another important point to consider about trading. Many buyers, especially professional buyers like purchasing agents, are worried about not getting the best deal possible. They have learned from experience that suppliers are often not disciplined in their pricing and that it's often the customer who pushes the hardest—not the most loyal or biggest customer—who gets the best price.

Buyers will push you on price to test you. If they push and you keep giving, that signals that you haven't reached your bottom price and that they should keep pushing. By developing and using trades, you can counter this pushing on price by buyers.

KEY TAKEAWAYS

- Professional buyers use games because the games are often an easy way to get suppliers to give away value.

- There are many different types of games that buyers may try to play with you.

- Preparation is key. Go back and understand the buying process, buying center, your value, and your trades.

- It's often helpful to get beyond what game the buyer is trying to play with you and ask why they are using the game.

- One strategy to deal with games if you are the incumbent is to educate the customer about the switching costs involved in moving from one supplier to another.

- Another strategy is to name the relationship the buyer is creating with you and be clear about what that means.

NOTES

1. www.brainyquote.com (accessed February 7, 2014).

2. C. Provines, "Professional Buyers' View of Suppliers" (Unpublished manuscript, 2013).

3. These tactics and counter moves are develop from the author's experience, interviews with procurement leaders, and B. Perdue and J. Summers "Purchasing Agents' Use of Negotiation Strategies" *Journal of Marketing Research* 28.2 (May 1991): 175–89.

4. P. Mitchell, "Maverick Spend: 12 Ways to Fix Internal Non-Compliance Beyond 'The Stick'" [Blog], Spendmatters.com, June 6, 2013, (accessed November 2, 2013).

5. Adapted from T. R. Lewis and Y. Huseyin, "Managing Switching Costs in Multiperiod Procurements with Strategic Buyers" (Working Paper 03-04, Duke University, Department of Economics, 2003).

6. E. Schneller, *The Value of Group Purchasing in the Health Care Supply Chain* (School of Health Administration and Policy, College of Business at Arizona State University, 2005).

PART V

APPENDICES

REIMBURSEMENT BASICS

Reimbursement is a critical area when it comes to selling and defending value. Reimbursement policy and payment levels can impact value perceptions and price sensitivity for supplies. It can be a very complicated area with differing rules for inpatient care, outpatient care, and diagnostic services. Further, each payer may have different reimbursement rules and policies. This chapter is meant to provide an overview of the basics of reimbursement.

TYPES OF REIMBURSEMENT SYSTEMS

Reimbursement is referred to in many ways. For the purposes of this book, reimbursement is defined as payment to a caregiver or asset owner by a payer or patient for healthcare services provided. A caregiver could be a physician, nurse, therapist, or other person involved in patient care. An asset owner is the person or organization who owns the assets where care is provided and can include hospitals, outpatient centers, doctors' offices, laboratories, and others. Depending on where in the world the care is provided, payment to the caregiver and asset owner can take a variety of forms.

There are a number of basic reimbursement systems operating today around the world for providers. The basic types of systems include capitated payments, fee for service, global budgets, per diems, and patient pay. Payment can vary based on where the supply item is used, who uses it, and how it is used. This appendix presents the basic systems, but realize that there are variants.

Capitated Payments

Capitated payment systems are reimbursement mechanisms whereby the caregiver or asset owner is reimbursed one fixed amount for the episode of care. For example, in the US, Medicare reimburses hospitals based on a diagnosis-related group (DRG) for inpatient care. This is a prospective payment system that covers all the costs of care, excluding physician fees. In this system, all patients who are given care in the inpatient setting fall into one of roughly 750 DRGs. The number of DRGs changes over time as procedures change, new technologies are introduced, and the system undergoes further refinements.

Each DRG has its own payment amount. The payment is determined through a complicated cost-based method and basically represents an average cost. Hospitals, therefore, have an incentive to reduce their costs below the "average" DRG payment to earn a profit. Many other developed countries, like Germany and France, have some form of a DRG system.

Fee for Service

Fee for service is a payment mechanism whereby the payer pays the hospital or physician a fixed amount for providing a service. For example, as part of a routine physical, a physician may order laboratory tests for a patient. In a fee-for-service environment, the laboratory would bill the payer for the lab tests that are performed. Much of physician reimbursement in the US for services provided is based on a fee-for-service payment mechanism.

Global Budgets

In some countries, the reimbursement system works on the basis of a global budget. In the simple form, the government provides a fixed "global budget" to the hospital or region to care for all patients in a given region. This budget then must be allocated by the hospital or region to pay for all of the services provided. The hospital is responsible for determining what services it will offer.

Per Diem

This payment method pays providers and caregivers a fixed amount per day. There are a number of variations. Sometimes there is a fixed payment for a procedure and a per diem rate for recovery days in the hospital. These mechanisms vary across markets, and the hospitals negotiate these payments directly with private insurers. In the US, roughly a third of hospital payments are from private payers, and one primary form of private pay reimbursement is per diem.[1]

Charges or Discounted Charges

Most hospitals, at least in the US, have something called a charge master. A charge master is a list of all the goods and services that could possibly be consumed in the delivery of care, along with a price for each of those goods and services. It is essentially a hospital price list. The items on the price list can range from one hour of operating room time to a bandage to a daily rate for a patient room. Some insurers negotiate a discounted charges contract with hospitals. These discounts can be in excess of 50 percent.[2]

Patient Pay

Last, there is patient pay. In some markets, healthcare is still largely funded by patients. Patients can purchase insurance or decide to simply fund the cost of care when the need arises. In many developing markets, patient pay represents the primary form of payment. In some developed markets, like the US, a small percentage of patients are patient pay either because they so choose or because they cannot afford insurance.

The type of system in which the supply or service is being used can have significant implications for price sensitivity and value. For example, if a new interventional cardiology technology is being launched, the company needs to think through the value and pricing carefully. The technology could have different value and price sensitivity if it is being launched into a patient pay versus a global budget market.

CODING, COVERAGE, AND PAYMENT

Reimbursement has three key elements. It is important to have a basic understanding of the three elements since each can have an impact on the customer's business and your value proposition. The three elements are coding, coverage, and payment. Each will be discussed in detail.

Coding

The first element of reimbursement is coding. Coding can be very complex, and it is not unusual for professional coders to specialize in just one area of coding such as in-vitro diagnostics coding or endovascular coding. Even within one area, such as in-vitro diagnostics, laboratory coding can vary widely between clinical chemistry and molecular diagnostics. In basic terms, coding is simply a means by which payers, caregivers, and asset owners communicate about what service was provided (procedure code) and why it was provided (diagnosis code).

As a simplified example, a physician may send a patient to have a CT scan for a suspicious lung mass that was previously spotted on an x-ray. In this case, the procedure code is the CT scan of the lung. The diagnosis code is a mass on lung. In the US, the CT scanner owner would bill the payer for the scan, and the physician who reads the scan may also bill. Coding becomes important for selling and pricing since it can dictate how payers think about and pay for services and the technologies used to provide care.

Coverage

The next element is coverage. Coverage simply means the payer can limit the reimbursement for or access to services that are provided to patients. Particularly for new technologies, it is not unusual for payers to not cover or to limit coverage. This is usually done because there is a lack of clinical evidence supporting the use of the technology.

In some countries, such as the United Kingdom, coverage decisions can also include an economic evaluation. The UK agency National Institute for Health and Clinical Excellence reviews and makes recommendations on the use and coverage of medical technologies and procedures. Other countries have similar technology assessment groups. In the US, some private payers use technology assessments that include both clinical and economic evaluation.

As an example, consider carotid artery stenting. Carotid artery stenting is a procedure and technology that was introduced about a decade ago. This procedure involves placing a self-expanding stent into the patient's carotid artery. A self-expanding stent is a tiny metal scaffold that expands when inserted into the patient's artery. It is used to clear a blockage in the artery. Prior to the development of this procedure, the standard of care was carotid artery surgery. This is a surgical procedure whereby the carotid artery is opened, cleaned out, and sutured shut. The stenting procedure is a less invasive procedure that uses catheter-based technology.

Although carotid artery stenting was a less invasive procedure, the issue with the new carotid artery stenting procedure was that it required a physician who is highly trained in catheter skills. A mistake in placement of the stent could mean that emboli or plaque could dislodge and be transported to the brain via the carotid artery. This could have significant adverse patient impact, which could include stroke.

Given the potential safety issues for the new procedure and based on clinical evidence, the Centers for Medicare and Medicaid Services (CMS) chose to limit coverage of the technology to a certain high-risk patient population at approval. So, based on clinical—and sometimes economic—evidence, payers can limit coverage to a subset of the market. This has to be considered when thinking through your selling and marketing strategies.[3]

In the US, the CMS bases coverage decisions on whether a procedure or therapy is reasonable and necessary. In evaluating whether a procedure, therapy, or technology is reasonable and necessary, CMS explicitly takes clinical evidence into account. This could lead to decisions to cover only certain patient populations. While economics are not explicitly considered in coverage decisions, it would be naïve to assume that the budget impact of a new technology, therapy, or procedure is not evaluated. This is particularly true for high-priced medical technologies. Thus a supplier facing a coverage decision should have some understanding of the potential budget impact of its technology.

Payment

Payment is the third element of reimbursement. Payment is the amount paid by the payer to the caregiver and asset owner for services rendered. There are a variety of systems and processes around the globe for determining payment amounts. For example, in the US inpatient Medicare payment system, hospitals are reimbursed via a DRG. In the US and other countries that use the DRG system, the DRG payment amount is often the reference hospitals look to when considering the value and price of existing or new technologies used for inpatient care.

Assessing Reimbursement Situation

A better understanding of the reimbursement implications for selling starts with a basic assessment of the reimbursement situation. In general, a healthcare supplier needs to:

1. *Understand site of service.* This simply means understanding where the technology will be used. Will it be used primarily in the hospital? Or is it a physician's office-based product?

2. *Identify target markets.* This means identifying the target countries and markets where the product or solution will likely be launched.

3. *Identify patient population.* The target patient population will drive value as well as other activities. Therefore, it is important to understand which patient population is the target for the product or solution.

4. *Determine payer mix.* What is the payer mix for the type of technology? Is it private pay or government funded?

5. *Evaluate reimbursement mechanics.* Is there currently coverage for the procedure, therapy, or diagnostic that the technology is used in? Are there any coding issues?

6. *Assess payment levels.* Are the payment levels adequate to cover the value and price of the supply item for the provider? Are caregivers adequately reimbursed for their services?

7. *Understand evidence requirements.* If changes are needed in coverage or payment levels, clinical and often economic evidence will be required. The supplier should be determining the evidence required to unlock reimbursement.

8. *Learn the customer's reimbursement quality incentives.* Under healthcare reform in the United States, there are many new incentives and programs in place. It's important that the supplier understand where the customer stands in terms of specific reimbursement programs and incentives.

CONCLUSION

In general, reimbursement is a complicated area that is growing more complicated with the introduction of healthcare reform in the US and other changes outside of the US. Therefore, it's best to rely on your internal reimbursement experts or to seek the expertise of qualified external experts when thinking about how your value proposition will be impacted by reimbursement rules, policies, and mechanisms. This appendix was intended to provide an overview of the basics.

NOTES

1. U. Reinhart, "The Pricing Of U.S. Hospital Services: Chaos Behind a Veil of Secrecy," *Health Affairs* 25.1 (2006): 57–69.

2. Ibid.

3. Decision Memo for Carotid Artery Stenting (CAG-00085R); www.cms.gov (accessed June 28, 2012).

BASICS OF ACCOUNTABLE CARE ORGANIZATIONS

As if healthcare wasn't complicated enough, healthcare reform in the United States ushered in a number of new payment models and incentives to different members of the healthcare system. Sorting through all of this can be difficult.

This is especially true for suppliers who sell to or through accountable care organizations (ACOs). ACOs are a new mechanism for the Center for Medicare and Medicaid Services (CMS) to find ways to take costs out and improve quality of care through care coordination. Understanding these new entities is critical for suppliers to successfully sell and defend value.

BASICS OF ACOs

Under the CMS healthcare reform, ACOs are new entities created to encourage healthcare providers such as physicians and hospitals to move from a fee-for-service to a population-based health model. ACOs are legal entities that sign an agreement with CMS to manage a Medicare population. The ACO is accountable for the costs and quality of managing the patients. This can include being at risk for the cost of managing the patient population.

There are some basic requirements and expectations for providers to participate:[1]

- Must manage a population of at least 5,000 traditional Medicare beneficiaries

- Achieve cost reductions and quality metric goals

- Have strong primary care model

- Use processes, information systems, and staff to coordinate care

- Implement programs for patient health management

- Use electronic medical records and data analytics to identify and make improvements

Once an organization elects to be an ACO and signs an agreement with Medicare, patients are assigned to that ACO. ACOs operate in a specific geographical region. Patients are assigned to an ACO based on their primary care physician's membership in the ACO. Since many people do not have a primary care physician, patients are also assigned based on where they have been receiving the bulk of their care.

Unlike managed care, patients don't sign up for but rather are assigned to an ACO. The patient is free to see whichever physician he or she chooses. Being part of the ACO does not by itself limit choice.

For example, a patient assigned to an ACO in Maine may decide to spend part of the winter in Florida. If the patient needs surgery while in Florida, the ACO in Maine is accountable for those costs and the care. However, the ACO in Maine cannot direct or limit the patient's choice of what hospital to go to or physician to see.

ACO ORGANIZATION STRUCTURE

Since ACOs coordinate care and manage patients, physicians are at the center of the ACO model. There are three primary types of ACOs. The first two are physician-based models. The third is a hospital–physician collaboration model.

- *Multi-specialty group practice (MSGP).* This is a self-organizing and self-governed physician practice organization. It is composed of multiple physician specialties. The physicians establish peer review of quality, utilization, and costs. There are often incentives in place for the physicians to achieve cost and quality goals.

- *Independent practice association (IPA).* This is a group of independent physicians. These groups typically have come together to negotiate rates and contracts with payers. These groups now leverage shared services, organize the financing and implementation of electronic medical records (EMR), and coordinate care and utilization.

- *Hospital–physician collaboration.* This could be a hospital or hospital system that joins forces with or employs physicians. The hospital collaborates with the physicians to coordinate care for the patients. Much like the IPA and MSGP, these new entities must coordinate care, and manage utilization.

All of these organization models may have some variations. These organizations may own, contract with, be owned by, or form joint ventures with other organizations. For example, a hospital system that doesn't employ physicians may engage in a joint venture with a physician practice.

Insurers can also play a part in this model. As an example, Collaborative Health Systems (CHS), a subsidiary of insurer Universal American Corp., is collaborating with over thirty physician-led ACOs. CHS provides the back-office function and care-coordination process. This includes analytics, reporting, and other administrative activities.[2]

MEDICARE ACO RISK MODELS

Risk is at the heart of the ACO model. Essentially, risk is transferred from the payer, in this case CMS, to the provider. The level of risk depends on the arrangement that the specific ACO chooses. An expenditure target is defined for the ACO. The costs included in the expenditure target include Medicare Part A (inpatient), Medicare Part B (outpatient), skilled nursing facility, and nursing home costs.

Organizations can choose which model to sign up for. Typically, organizations will choose a model based on the level of risk they are willing to assume, their experience in managing population health, and the infrastructure that is in place to coordinate care and manage risk. There are three levels of risk an ACO could choose:

- *Pioneer ACOs.* This is designed for organizations that have experience and infrastructure in place to coordinate care and manage population health. This model is intended for organizations that can quickly transition from sharing savings to a population-health-based payment. For the first two years, the ACO would participate in a shared savings and loss model. In the third year, ACOs that are successful would be eligible to move to a per-beneficiary per-month payment model.[3]

- *Two-sided shared savings model.* This is designed for organizations that want to move from fee-for-service to population-based health. In this model, providers are paid under the traditional fee-for-service Medicare reimbursement. However, they are at risk for costs that exceed an expenditure target and are rewarded for costs below the expenditure target.[4]

- *One-sided shared savings model.* This is designed for organizations that want to gain experience with risk. Providers are paid under the traditional fee-for-service Medicare reimbursement. However, they are rewarded for costs below an expenditure target.[5]

ACOs AND YOUR VALUE PROPOSITION

For suppliers of goods and services, the key is to understand how the ACO will view your solution. A solution that creates value for one type of ACO may create little value for another type of ACO. Likewise, a solution that creates value for a hospital may create little or no value for an ACO.

For example, you might be selling a solution that reduces in-hospital costs. Let's say you have a new drug or device that significantly reduces length of stay. This would be valuable for the hospital. An ACO that is a hospital–physician collaboration would find value in the solution. However, a physician-led ACO with no financial interest in the hospital would find no value in the solution.

One simple way to think about the ACO business models and your value proposition is to consider how the ACO makes money. Physician-led ACOs make money by keeping people out of the ER and hospital.[6] Many physician-led ACOs are creating new care pathways and their own outpatient facilities to keep patients out of the ER and hospital.

These physician-led ACOs also make money by reducing unnecessary diagnostics and services. Many are implementing or have implemented sophisticated systems to track utilization of services by physician.[7] Basically, these ACOs make money by keeping patients healthy and out of expensive sites of service.

On the other hand, a hospital–physician collaboration ACO may have different incentives because of their business model. In this model, revenue for the hospital from performing a procedure, test, or service is actually a cost to the ACO. For example, when the hospital cares for a patient in the inpatient setting, the hospital is paid a DRG payment. This DRG payment counts as revenue for the hospital, but as cost for the ACO.

Hospitals want to bill volume while minimizing hospital-related costs. A physician-led ACO is incentivized to reduce unnecessary tests and procedures, and to keep people out of the hospital. A hospital–physician ACO is focused on minimizing total costs across the continuum of care.

CONCLUSION

ACOs are an important new stakeholder in care delivery in the United States. Whether ACOs survive or morph into a different type of entity or model is not known. However, they do bring a new level of complexity for healthcare suppliers to understand and communicate their value proposition. It's important that the supplier clearly understand how its product or solution impacts this stakeholder. The impact and perceived value may differ depending on the form of ACO and its business structure.

NOTES

1. See CMS.gov for more information.

2. D. Manos, "Collaborative Health Systems Collaborates with 15 More ACOs, Brings Total to 31," Healthcareitnews.com, January 15, 2013 (accessed November 2, 2013).

3. See CMS ACO factsheet, CMS.gov.

4. G. Burke, *Moving Towards Accountable Care in New York* (United Hospital Fund, 2013).

5. Ibid.

6. Ibid.

7. Ibid.

INDEX

V

W

ABOUT THE COVER

According to Wikipedia, the figure of the two intertwined serpents and staff, sometimes surmounted by wings, is called the caduceus. It comes from Greek mythology, and one of its original meanings was related to commerce and negotiation. In the United States, the symbol is used, some say incorrectly, by many commercial healthcare organizations. In Greek mythology, the symbol of medicine or healing is the Rod of Asclepius, which has one serpent entwining a rod. The Caduceus's association with healthcare in the US dates back to 1902, when the US Army Medical Corps adopted the symbol for its insignia. Since then, it has been associated with healthcare or medicine in the US. So a symbol with mixed meaning—commerce for some and healthcare for others—is appropriate, in either case, for this book. The cover design is meant to capture healthcare, growth, and clarity of value. The idea and design are by Kliment Korobar of Klidesign, from the crowdspring.com design contest platform.

ABOUT THE AUTHOR

Christopher Provines has over twenty-four years of global healthcare experience. He began his career in hospital finance and reimbursement. After graduate school, he joined Johnson & Johnson and later moved to Siemens Healthcare. His roles have included vice-president-level positions at both companies.

He has extensive global experience in a variety of functions, including strategic pricing, reimbursement, health outcomes, finance, procurement, commercial excellence, key account management, and business improvement. He is a world-leading thought leader in selling, defending, and capturing value in healthcare. He is an advisor to many of the world's leading medical technology and pharmaceutical companies.

Chris has written many papers, articles, book chapters, and books. He is on the board of advisors for the Professional Pricing Society and is an award-winning adjunct professor at Rutgers University, where he teaches in the Supply Chain Management and Marketing Sciences Department. His research interests include the transformation of healthcare supply chains and the implications for suppliers. Chris earned his MBA from Rutgers University.